YOUTH VOLLEYBALL DRILLS

COLLECTION 1

Copyright © 2018 The Art of Coaching Volleyball, LLC

All rights reserved. This book or any portion thereof may not be reproduced or used in any manner whatsoever without the express written permission of the publisher except for the use of brief quotations in a book review.

Printed in the United States of America

First Printing, 2018

ISBN 978-0-9989765-6-3

Published by The Art of Coaching Volleyball, LLC
3720 SW 141st Avenue, Suite 209
Beaverton, OR 97005

www.theartofcoachingvolleyball.com

Introduction
Cary Wendell Wallin, 949 Volleyball Club

There's nothing more rewarding than coaching young volleyball players. They learn every time they're in the gym, and the "light bulb" moments are fun to be a part of.

As coaches of these age groups, it's our job to give players solid fundamental skills that they can carry with them for the rest of their volleyball playing days. The purpose of this drill book is to provide coaches with creative ways to work on improving the basic skills of volleyball while also keeping things fun and interesting for young players. There's so much to love about volleyball. The drills in this book highlight that enjoyment and help players develop a strong command of the game's fundamentals.

As someone who has coached young volleyball athletes for many years, I'd like to share a few teaching points that have worked for me:

- **Preparing practice plans** and considering adjustments for when players miss practice is extremely worthwhile. This will make your time in the gym more fun and productive.

- Choose **two or three things to focus on** during practice that you can share with the team before practice starts.

- Set aside time during practice for **quality individual reps** that can then be incorporated into team drills.

- For some drills, **players can and should initiate the ball.** Other times, the coach needs to do it to ensure a more controlled learning opportunity. It's always a good idea to start simple and add more complexity as the players develop stronger skills.

- Look to **maximize the gym space available** to you by using a wall as a net for setting reps or a corner of the gym for defense. If you have an assistant coach, consider breaking up into rotating stations to maximize repetitions and reduce time spent standing in long lines.

- **Don't be afraid to be a little silly** at times with this age group. Use fun warm-ups (shared in this book), creative competition consequences (like wheelbarrow races), and plan practices that have a theme – like dress-up days or crazy hair days.

- Remember, **competition always makes things more interesting** and keeps players engaged. Instead of just going through free-ball reps, have two groups racing to see who can get to 10 good free-ball passes first. Instead of just running sprints, make it a relay race. Instead of just serving, play the game of "Jailbreak," which you'll find on page 28.

Introduction
Cary Wendell Wallin, 949 Volleyball Club

- **Team bonding is also important.** If you see the same players always partnering up, set them up for partner work and then rotate everyone at the net so they work with different teammates. Parents can host team get-togethers outside of tournaments to facilitate team bonding. The more a team bonds, the better the players will compete together and the more they will enjoy the season.

- **Communication is key at this age.** Tightness often makes young players freeze up and stop talking, and then the wheels come off the bus. Inexperienced players still don't quite know which balls they should step in and take, and that can cause hesitation. The more players talk about what is happening on the court, the fewer unforced errors the team will experience, and the faster they will improve as individuals and as a team. The trick is finding the right balance between pushing them and making sure you're building confidence and a strong skill set for volleyball and life.

I've found that 12-and-unders are the most rewarding age to coach. Tournament success at this age doesn't always mean winning, which you could do by teaching your kids to bump the ball over on the first try and rely on the other team to make mistakes. It's much better to measure competition success by how much your young athletes play like they do in practice. This helps them prioritize the important stuff – like learning the rhythm of the game and carrying over skills they learned from drills into tournament play. This may not always lead to a win, but it will help them become better volleyball players.

With an abundance of patience, a sprinkle of humor, and the drills in this book, you'll have the right recipe to teach your kids the sport of volleyball. As they play with passion and learn to communicate on and off the court, they will ultimately love this amazing sport … and then you will have truly mastered the art of coaching young volleyball players.

Cary Wendall Wallin
Former NCAA Player of the Year at Stanford
Coach at 949 Volleyball Club in San Juan Capistrano, CA

Introduction
How to Use Your Youth Volleyball Drill Book

The Youth Volleyball Drill Book has been developed to provide coaches and teachers at the youth level with a comprehensive tool for teaching volleyball skills and practicing game situations.

The drills in this book were provided by a variety of youth volleyball coaches, including Deborah Newkirk (COACH 'EM UP), Cary Wendell Wallin (949 VBC), Ruth Nelson (BYOP®) and Leisa Rosen (University of Michigan).

This book contains drills for:

- Warm-ups
- Serving
- Passing
- Setting

- Attacking
- Defense
- Ball Control
- Team Situations

Drills in this book are labeled to make it as easy as possible for you, the coach, to choose the drills that are right for your team and to run them as effectively as possible. Drill descriptions are broken up into four main parts: Difficulty, How it works, Variations and Requirements.

Difficulty:

Below each drill's title you will find a difficulty rating of one, two or three dots. These dots are designed to give you an idea of how difficult the drill will be for players to execute.

● ○ ○   Drills to use with any level of youth player

● ● ○   Drills for players with some previous skill training

● ● ●   Drills for advanced youth players

Drills with a **one-dot rating** are good to use with any level of youth player. These drills include basic movement patterns and games that can be modified to suit a player's skill level (i.e. serving from the 10-foot line instead of the baseline), and they often involve the coach initiating the ball to remove unnecessary variables (i.e. a player's toss). A lot of these drills work on developing the fundamentals while taking the net out of play.

Drills with a **two-dot rating** are slightly more advanced in that they involve more player movement, over-the-net play, partner-work and are more often player-initiated. Players will be more successful in these drills if they have had some prior skill instruction.

Drills with a **three-dot rating** will work best with advanced youth players who have had a lot of prior skill training. These drills include over-the-net play, continuous drills, team drills and game-like situations and scoring.

Table of Contents

1 Drill Key

3 Warm-up Drills

4	Agility Ladder Drills	● ○ ○
4	Blocking Footwork Drill	● ● ○
5	Box Steps	● ○ ○
6	Coach's Choice	● ● ○
7	Communication Drill	● ● ○
8	Four Muscle Memory Throws	● ○ ○
9	Hitting Footwork Drill	● ○ ○
9	Jab-Step Progression Drill	● ○ ○
10	Partner Run-Through	● ● ○
11	Warm-up Footwork Drill	● ○ ○
12	Warm-up Movement Game	● ○ ○

19 Serving Drills

20	10 in 30 Drill	● ● ○
21	8 in 8 Drill	● ● ○
22	Amoeba	● ○ ○
24	Baseline Throws	● ○ ○
25	Coach's Toss Serving	● ○ ○
26	Dead Fish	● ○ ○
27	Forty Serves	● ● ○
28	Jailbreak	● ○ ○
29	Mock Serving Drill	● ○ ○
30	Serve-a-Thon	● ● ○
31	Serving Practice Drill	● ○ ○
32	Snake	● ○ ○
33	Spiderweb	● ○ ○
34	Spot Serving Drill	● ● ●
35	Three Ball Speed Serve	● ● ○
36	Three Deep Drill	● ● ●
37	Three Short, Three Deep Drill	● ● ●
38	Touchdown Serves	● ○ ○
39	Water Break Drill	● ● ●
40	Won It, Lost It, Tied It	● ● ○

Table of Contents

45 Passing Drills

46	Chair Passing	●●○
47	Fill the Void	●●●
48	Four Corners	●●●
49	Four Player Pass and Switch	●●●
50	Free Ball 1,2,3 Drill	●○○
51	Free Ball Footwork Drill	●●○
52	Handle the Heat Drill	●●○
53	Hips to the Ball	●○○
54	One-Knee Passing Drill	●○○
55	Partner Ball Rolls	●○○
56	Partner Pass and Set Drill	●●○
57	Partner Passing	●●○
58	Pass and Switch Drill	●●●
59	Pass and Turn Drill	●○○
60	Passing Footwork on Command	●○○
61	Pretzel Drill	●●○
62	Queen of the Throne	●●●
63	Run-Through Drill	●●○
64	Serve Receive Wave Drill	●●●
65	Shuffle Back Passing	●●○
66	Shuffle, Shuffle, Freeze Dance	●○○
67	Step-Hop Drill	●●○
68	Target Spots	●●○
69	Team Popcorn Drill	●●○
70	Three-Man Passing	●●○
71	Toss, Claim, Catch Drill	●○○
72	Wall Touch Passing	●●○

77 Setting Drills

78	Basketball Keys Drill	●●●
79	Beginner Setting Drills	●○○
80	Ground Setting Drill	●○○
81	Half-Star Setting Drill	●●●
82	Partner Knee Work	●●○
83	Partner Setting Drill	●○○
84	Rapid Fire Setting	●●○

Table of Contents

85	S5 Target Sets	●●●
86	Setter Training Progression	●●○
87	Setter's Call Drill	●●●
88	Setting Fan Drill	●●○
89	Setting Lines	●●○
90	Stability Ball Drill	●●○
91	Star Footwork Patterns	●●●
92	Target Setting	●●●
93	Tennis Ball Setting	●○○
94	Triangle Hand Placement Drill	●○○

99 Attacking Drills

100	Alligator Attacks	●●○
101	Box Hitting Drill	●○○
102	Hitting Jail Break	●●○
103	Net Down Balls Drill	●●○
104	Red, White, and Blue Hitting Drill	●●○
105	Reds and Outsides Hitting	●●○
106	Team Hitting Drill	●●○
107	Three Hits Goal	●●○
108	Wall Spiking Drill	●○○

113 Defense Drills

114	Blocker Wall	●●●
115	Bounce and Chase Drill	●●○
116	Chase Drill	●●○
117	Cone Agility Drill	●○○
118	Dig to Boxes	●●○
119	Digging Challenge	●●●
120	Elastic Digging Drill	●●○
121	Knockout Digging Drill	●●○
122	Step and Stick	●○○
123	Ten to Win	●●○
124	Tennis Ball Touch	●○○
125	Toss and Collapse Drill	●●○

131 Ball Control Drills

| 132 | 1-on-1 Competitive Drill | ●●● |
| 133 | Air Popcorn Machine | ●○○ |

Table of Contents

134	Big Kernel, Little Kernel	●●○
135	Butterfly	●●●
136	Funny Pepper	●●○
137	Over-the-Net Pepper	●●●
138	Partner Tennis Ball Tosses	●○○
139	Patterns Drill	●●○
140	Popcorn Series	●●○
141	Rotating Group Pepper	●●●
142	Ten to Kill	●●●
143	Two Ball Pepper	●●●
144	Volleyball Jog	●●○

149 Team Drills

150	7-Up	●●○
151	Bad Pass, Good Save	●●○
152	Catch, Toss, Spike Game	●●○
153	Free Ball, Free Ball, Free Ball, Attack	●●●
154	Free Ball, Free Ball, Free Ball, Wash	●●●
155	Golden Egg Drill	●●○
156	Mini Player Tournament	●●●
157	Newcomb Game	●●○
158	Queens of the Court	●●○
159	Set the Setter	●●○
160	Speed Ball	●●○

Drill Key

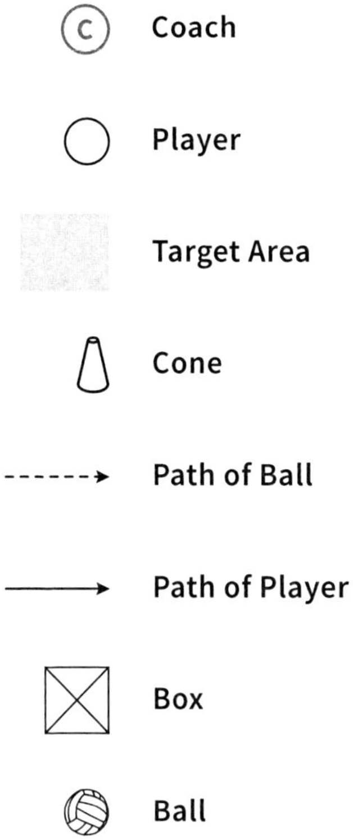

⊙ Coach

◯ Player

▨ Target Area

⌂ Cone

-----> Path of Ball

——→ Path of Player

⊠ Box

⚽ Ball

Warm-up Drills

Warm-up
Agility Ladder Drills

Difficulty: ● ○ ○

How it works: These ladder drills can be used to start each day of a youth camp or practice. To begin, place an agility ladder on the floor. Players line up and take turns moving quickly down the ladder using one of three jumping techniques:

- **One in the hole:** Players place one foot in each space
- **Two in the hole:** Players place both feet, one at a time, in each space
- **Hopscotch:** Players jump with two feet together in each space, then two feet split on the outside of the ladder

Variations: To make these drills competitive, set up two or three ladders and have players race.

Requirements: One or more players, at least one ladder and 10-20 feet of floor space

Blocking Footwork Drill

Difficulty: ● ● ○

How it works: To practice blocking arm movement, players spread out across the court. They assume a blocking ready position with a crouched lower body, hands spread, arms in front of the chest and elbows in tight. On the coach's command, players jump and block with arms extended diagonally over an imaginary net.

To practice traditional blocking footwork, players move using one of the following techniques on the coach's command:

- **2-step:** Take one shuffle step right and jump, then one shuffle step left and jump
- **3-step:** Take two shuffle steps right and jump, then two shuffle steps left and jump
- **4-step:** Turn right, run, step and jump, then turn left, run, step and jump

Requirements: Six or more players, a coach and a half court

Warm-up
Box Steps

Difficulty: ● ○ ○

How it works: To practice passing footwork movement, players spread out across the court. They assume a ready passing position with a crouched lower body and arms relaxed in front of the body. On the coach's command, players move using one of the following techniques:

- Box step right
    1. Take one step to the right side with the right foot followed by a shuffle step
    2. Take one step back leading with the left foot followed by a shuffle step
    3. Take one step to the left side with the left foot followed by a shuffle step
    4. Take one step forward with the left foot followed by a shuffle step

- Box step left
    1. Take one step to the left side with the left foot followed by a shuffle step
    2. Take one step back leading with the right foot followed by a shuffle step
    3. Take one step to the right side with the right foot followed by a shuffle step
    4. Take one step forward with the right foot followed by a shuffle step

Requirements: Six or more players, a coach and a half court

Warm-up
Coach's Choice

Difficulty: ● ● ○

How it works: One player starts at the 15-foot line in defensive position, arms at 90 degrees. The players job is to successfully handle whatever the coach standing at the net throws at them. This could be a short ball requiring a run-through play, a hard-driven spike that needs to dug, or a deep lob to chase down. As the coach sends the ball their way, players go to release position, then make a play on the ball. Repeat several times with different shot types.

Requirements: One or more players, a coach, a cart of balls and a half court

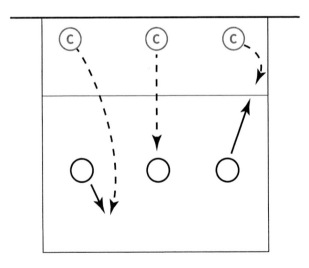

Warm-up
Communication Drill

Difficulty: ● ● ○

How it works: Assemble six players per side with three at the net and three in the back court. Have front and back row players partner up and set the ball back and forth at antenna height.

To promote better concentration, have one player act as the "metronome." They set the tempo and direct the play by shouting "toss" or "set" when they touch the ball. All players should try to match the metronome player's tempo.

Requirements: Six or more players in partners, a coach, one ball per pair and a full court

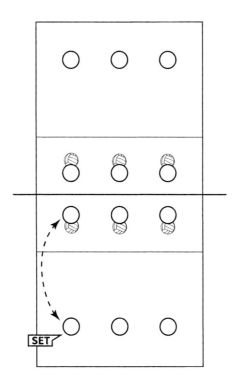

Warm-up
Four Muscle Memory Throws

Difficulty: ● ○ ○

How it works: There are four muscle-memory throws:
1. **Two Thumbs by the Thighs:** Players, positioned with a partner, throw for warm-up and also for developing essential movements in overhand serving, hitting, and hip rotation. Two Thumbs by the Thighs has partners bouncing the ball hard once to the floor - playing catch - back and forth.
2. **Elbow by the Eye:** Players pause and adjust their throwing arm to get the throwing arm elbow "by the eye." As they throw with the opposite foot forward, the coach reminds players of the opening and closing of their hips. Players throw from high to low, meaning wrist snap at the release, aiming for the receiving partner's knee pads.
3. **Back to Your Partner:** Partners face away from each other and step forward, with either foot to switch it up, arching the back and "throwing their chest to the ceiling" and holding their arms way up high pose.
4. **Two Slaps and a Down Ball:** Two big open hand "slappy" sounds on the ball followed by a down ball to their partner. The ball bounces once. Remind players in this "throw" to not toss the ball, but to hit it out of their own hand or after a very small toss.

Requirements: Two or more players, one ball per pair and a half court

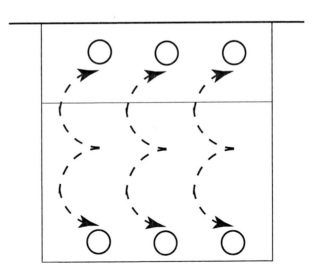

Check out the youth drill videos we have online!

Warm-up
Hitting Footwork Drill

Difficulty: ● ○ ○

How it works:
- **Drill #1:** To practice hitting footwork, players spread out across the court and get into starting position: right foot back, arms relaxed in front and weight on the left side of the body. To start the hitting approach, take one step with the right foot swinging the left arm forward, then a second step with the left foot swinging the right arm forward. On the third step, place the right foot forward with the right toe facing slightly toward the right and swing both arms back to generate momentum, then step with the left foot and drive the body and arms upward. Land in a blocking position with body crouched and hands facing the net at chest height.

- **Drill #2:** To retreat from left front and transition into attack, turn to the right and take four steps toward the back court, then pivot in the air to face the net again. Repeat the hitting approach and land in blocking position.

- **Drill #3:** To go from serve receive into attack, mimic a pass with arms angled toward the setter, shuffle step to the left a few times, then take a hitting approach and land in blocking position.

Requirements: One or more players and a half court

Jab-Step Progression Drill

Difficulty: ● ○ ○

How it works: To practice passing arm and footwork movement, players spread out across the court. They assume a ready passing position with a crouched lower body and arms at 90 degrees in front of the body. On the coach's command, players move using one of the following techniques:

- **Jab-step right:** Take one step forward with the right foot, extend the arms to pass then angle the shoulders and platform to the right toward an imaginary net. Return to starting position.

- **Jab-step left:** Take one step forward with the left foot, extend the arms to pass then angle the shoulders and platform to the left toward an imaginary net. Return to starting position.

Requirements: Six or more players, a coach and a half court

www.theartofcoachingvolleyball.com/youthdb1

Warm-up
Partner Run-Through

Difficulty: ● ● ○

How it works: Have players partner up with one player at the endline and the other at the net with a ball. Player 1 at the net lobs the ball vertically in front of the 10-foot (3 m) line. Player 2 runs through and plays the ball up, then catches it. Next, player 1 lobs the ball toward the endline, forcing player 2 to chase it down and pass it back over their shoulder to player 1 who is trailing. Each time, player 1 should give player 2 verbal direction by calling "ball, ball, ball."

Requirements: Two or more players in partners, one ball per pair and a half court

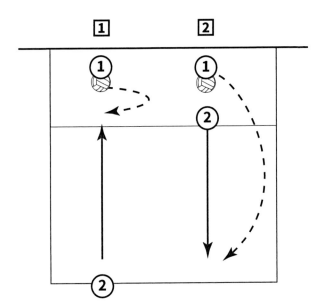

Warm-up
Warm-up Footwork Drill

Difficulty: ● ○ ○

How it works: Players line up along the right sideline. The first player enters the court at the right front position and shuffles in a zigzag pattern across the court, moving back and forth between the net and the 10-foot (3 m) line.

Next, players repeat the drill using a run-shuffle pattern where they run from right front to the 10-foot (3 m) line, then shuffle back to the net, repeating this pattern all the way across the court.

Requirements: Three or more players and a half court

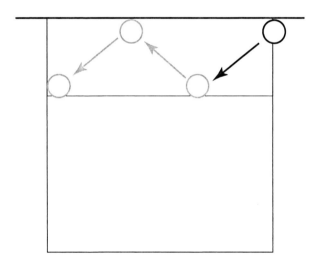

Warm-up
Warm-up Movement Game

Difficulty: ● ○ ○

How it works: In this move-your-feet drill for four to six players (diagram 1), position two players on each side of the net and start the action by tossing one ball into play. The goal is to catch the ball, hold it for one second, then toss it to a partner who holds it for one second before tossing it over the net. When an error occurs, the losing pair run off the court and are replaced by two new players.

In the next variation (diagram 2), the first player passes the ball to the second player, who catches and throws the ball over the net. The third variation has three players per side, each of whom must catch and throw the ball.

Next (diagram 3), while still having three contacts per side, the first player passes or sets before the next two catch and throw. With each variation, the players on the losing side run off and are replaced by new players.

Variations: Make the court as big or small as needed for the level of play. To work on communication, you can require players to call the name of the person they plan to throw to. For more skilled players, try setting the first ball, catching the second and hitting the third.

Requirements: Four to six players, a cart of balls, a coach and a full court

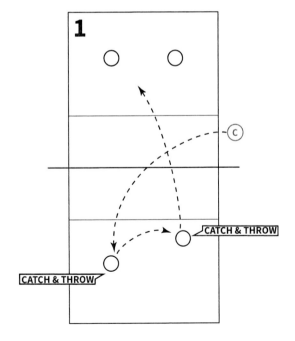

Check out the youth drill videos we have online!

Warm-up
Warm-up Movement Game

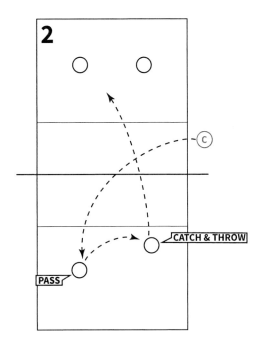

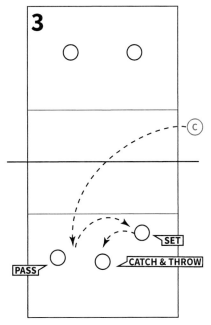

www.theartofcoachingvolleyball.com/youthdb1

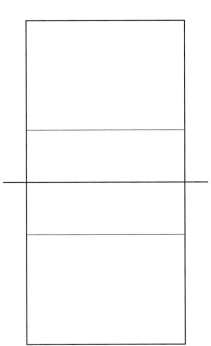

17

Serving Drills

Serving
10 in 30 Drill

Difficulty: ● ● ○

How it works: All players work hard to add a point to the team score by making their serves. The coach puts a certain amount of time on the clock and players work hard to successfully get the team goal that is set by the coach. For example, the coach may challenge a team to get 10 serves over in 30 seconds. Players are equally divided on each end and all volleyballs are out to use for quick serving. Players yell out, "One!" "Two!" "Three!" etc., counting loudly as each serve goes over the net.

Requirements: Six or more players, a coach, a cart of balls and a full court

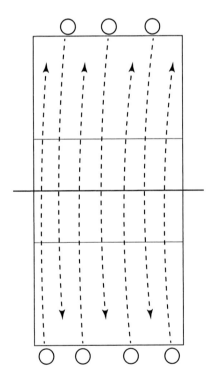

Serving
8 in 8 Drill

Difficulty: ● ● ○

How it works: Players are divided equally on both service baselines. In eight attempts, counted out by the coach, players work to successfully serve eight consecutive volleyballs over the net and in. This may not happen the first time, but it's a good team goal. All players work together as the coach counts the good serves. Eight serves in eight minutes may work better for some initial success if eight attempts is too tough.

Requirements: Six or more players, a coach, a cart of balls and a full court

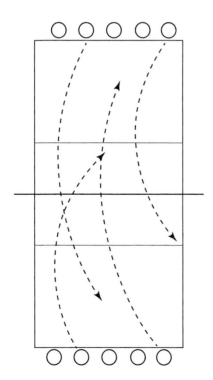

Serving
Amoeba

Difficulty: ● ○ ○

How it works: Start with a line of players along the endline or wherever players are capable of serving from, one ball per player. One at a time, players serve underhand. The first server serves to a single player on the other side of the net who lets the ball go through a hoop she makes with her arms. As soon as the serve crosses the net, the server charges under and joins hands with the other player(s) to form a larger hoop. The receiving side moves as a unit to "hoop" the serve. As more players are added, the circle grows quite large as the drill progresses. Continue until all players have served.

Variations: Run the drill on two courts with teams competing to "hoop" all their serves first. As players work through their fears of being hit by a ball, coaches lend support and help the players celebrate in a fun environment.

Requirements: Ten to 12 players, a cart of balls and a full court

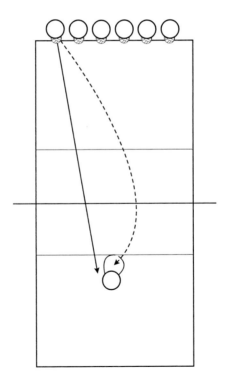

Check out the youth drill videos we have online!

Serving
Amoeba

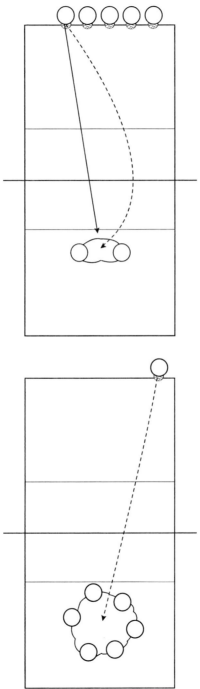

Serving
Baseline Throws

Difficulty: ● ○ ○

How it works: To help develop a fast striking arm, quick rotating hips, and a high elbow release or contact point, players throw from the baseline (tennis balls work best), over the net and into designated areas with various point values. Players are encouraged to throw with a higher than normal arm, and the coach can make it a challenge by tallying individual scores or a team personal best.

Variations: Putting two teams against each other and allowing three throws each can make things more competitive and fun too.

Requirements: Six or more players, a coach, two carts of balls and a full court

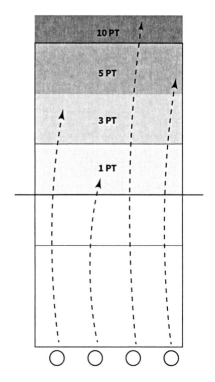

Serving
Coach's Toss Serving

Difficulty: ● ○ ○

How it works: To eliminate the one thing that many times gets in the way of that overhand serve--the toss-- let's have the coach toss for the players. Players form two lines or a line per coach. The coach positions the volleyball out in front of the server's hitting shoulder. The player has his or her striking hand on top of the ball, relaxed. When the coach says, "Pull," the player pulls their hand back over their head and shoulder area with four fingertips facing the ceiling. The player does not have their tossing hand anywhere near the ball. The player serves the toss. Players shag their balls and return to the serving lines.

Requirements: Six or more players, one to two coaches, one to two carts of balls, and a full court

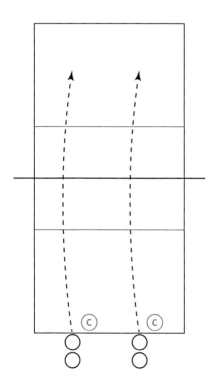

www.theartofcoachingvolleyball.com/youthdb1   25

Serving
Dead Fish

Difficulty: ● ○ ○

How it works: A coach divides the team into two even groups along the endlines or wherever players are capable of serving from. On the coach's whistle, all fish start serving. If a fish misses their serve, that server dips under the net to the other side's 10-foot (3 m) line and sits criss-cross. That player is now a "dead fish" (DF). Live fish are trying to serve to their dead fish teammates because if a dead fish can catch a teammate's serve, they get to return to the live fish side. All fish keep serving to save and bring back their dead fish until all fish are dead. The side with the most live fish at the end of a certain time wins! If the team is playing without a clock/time, play until one side are all dead fish, the winning fish are those with a minimum of one standing.

Requirements: Six or more players, a coach, two carts of balls and a full court

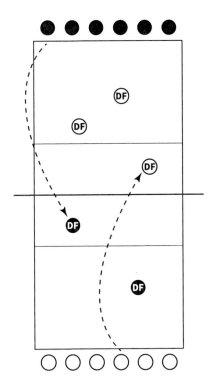

26   Check out the youth drill videos we have online!

Serving
Forty Serves

Difficulty: ● ● ○

How it works: The coach divides the team in either two or four groups. Ideally, this game is played on two courts, but it can easily be played on one. When the game begins, the teams attempt to get as many serves over as possible. They earn 1 point per made serve, up to 10 points. After 10 points, the serving team moves to the first open baseline. Once 10 more team serves are made, the team runs to the next open service area. Making 10 team serves from four different baselines gets you to 40 serves, and 40 wins the game! If you are only playing on one court, teams can serve five from both ends twice, for a game total of 20.

Requirements: Six or more players, a coach, two carts of balls and one to two full courts

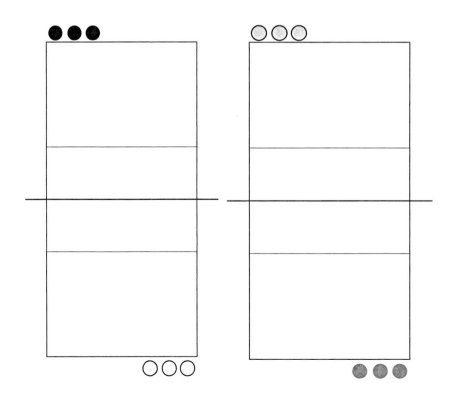

Serving
Jailbreak

Difficulty: ● ○ ○

How it works: All players line up along the endline, or wherever players are capable of serving from, on the "law-abiding citizens" side of the net. When a serve is missed, the player who missed is sent off to jail. There are two ways a player can get out of jail: a coach yells, "Jailbreak!" or a player claims a serve and catches it. If a player catches the volleyball from jail, he or she goes back to the serving side and the player whose ball was caught goes to jail.

Requirements: Six or more players, a coach, a cart of balls and a full court

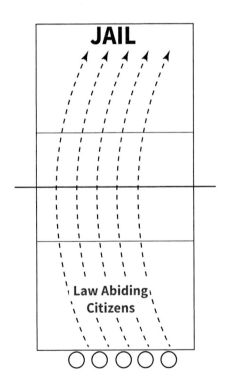

Serving
Mock Serving Drill

Difficulty: ● ○ ○

How it works: Partners stand across the net from each other, starting at the 10-foot (3 m) line. The receiving partner is a big target with hands up, ready to catch. Players continue serving back and forth until the coach chooses to advance the drill. Players are then asked to take one step back and continue serving again.

Requirements: Six or more players, one ball per pair and a full court

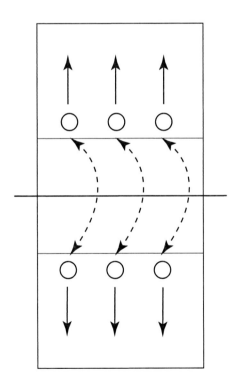

Serving
Serve-a-Thon

Difficulty: ● ● ○

How it works: The coach divides the team into two even groups. These two serving teams start on the baseline with a volleyball, ready to serve. With 5 minutes on the clock, players realistically pledge out loud the number of serves they can successfully get in. With individual and team projections set, the coach starts the drill and players quickly serve and go get another ball to serve, doing their best to meet their realistic goal. The players may be under their projected number but cannot be over. If the player "pledged" 15 made serves in the 5-minute time allowed and they successfully make 16, then only the pledged number applies to their score. Players usually under pledge, so they can feel certain to apply their score.

Variations: For a simpler, less competitive variation, have players pledge and get an entire team projected score and see what they ended up actually getting. Do the drill a second time being more realistic or raising the bar.

Requirements: Six or more players, a coach, and a full court

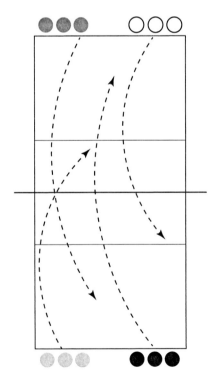

Serving
Serving Practice Drill

Difficulty: ● ○ ○

How it works: Each player gets a ball and spreads out in open space. From a kneeling position, players pin the ball to the floor repeatedly by pulling their wrists back, spreading their fingers wide and contacting the ball with the heel of their hands.

Variations: Players can perform this drill against the wall, pinning the ball against the hard surface, keeping their wrists firm on contact. In the "double pin" variation, players pin the ball once against the wall, let it fall a few inches, then pin it against the wall again. A third variation is the knee serve. Players start about 10 feet (3 m) away from the wall, then serve the ball against it from a kneeling position. They must serve hard enough so the ball rebounds to a coach-designated location. This works best with a partner who can shag and return the ball to the server. Move players away from the wall even more to practice a deeper serve.

Requirements: One or more players, one ball per player and a full court

Serving
Snake

Difficulty: ● ○ ○

How it works: Split your players in half and have one half stand on one side ready to serve (S) from the endline, or wherever players are capable of serving from. The other players line up along the endline acting as targets for the servers (T). The target players snake their way slowly back and forth toward the net. The target players may not duck out of the way, but instead must allow the ball to contact them. A player who is hit exits the court, leaving the remaining target players behind. The ultimate goal: be the last player left on the target side.

Requirements: Ten to 12 players, a cart of balls and a full court

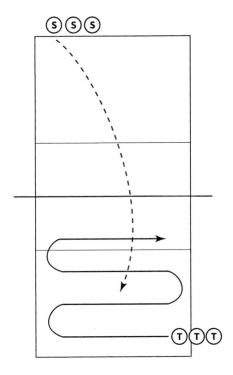

Serving
Spiderweb

Difficulty: ● ○ ○

How it works: The spiderweb is on one side of the floor anywhere inbounds but behind the 10-foot (3 m) line. A coach picks a couple of "serving spiders" to begin serving the spider eggs (volleyballs) over the net line from the endline or wherever players are capable of serving from. The "serving spiders" serve into the web full of spiders. When a serving spider hits a spider directly, the hit spider becomes a serving spider. When all spiders are serving and the game is down to the last two or three spiders still in the web, the web spiders become the new serving spiders, starting a new game.

Requirements: Six or more players, a coach, a cart of balls and a full court

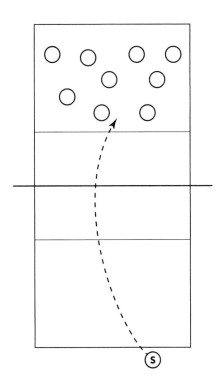

Serving
Spot Serving Drill

Difficulty: ● ● ●

How it works: All players line up on one baseline, ready to serve. With five boxes or chairs set up to symbolize players, hula hoops or cones are placed in the target spaces between the chairs. Players serve, aiming for cones or hula hoops while avoiding the chairs. This teaches the lesson that we want opponents to move to get to a serve. In other words, we don't serve to players, we serve to spaces between players.

Requirements: Six or more players, five chairs or boxes, five hula hoops or cones, a coach, a cart of balls and a full court

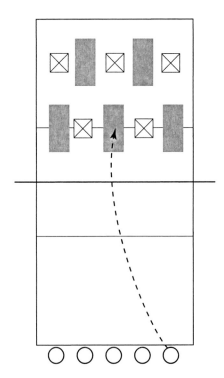

Serving
Three Ball Speed Serve

Difficulty: ● ● ○

How it works: Three balls are placed on the floor: one at the 10-foot (3 m) line with a server, one at the halfway point on the same side of the net, and one on the baseline. The server moves from ball to ball, starting at the closest one to the net. Servers serve one ball and quickly go to the next and then to the third ball. The goal is for players to not over think, but just pick up the ball and serve, serve, serve.

Requirements: Three or more players, at least three balls and a full court

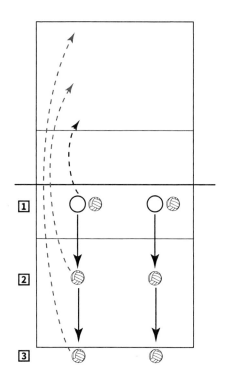

www.theartofcoachingvolleyball.com/youthdb1   35

Serving
Three Deep Drill

Difficulty: ● ● ●

How it works: Players serve as a team, and all players are positioned on one baseline. Servers serve deep. The team tries to get three deep serves in a row. Once the first serve lands in either zone 1, 6 or 5, two more must land deep to win the drill.

Requirements: Six or more players, a cart of balls and a full court

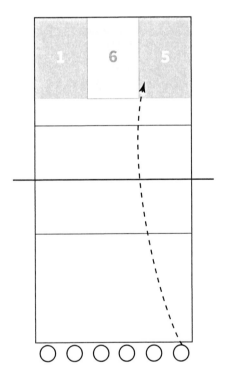

Serving
Three Short, Three Deep Drill

Difficulty: ● ● ●

How it works: The coach divides the group in two and places a group on each of the two baselines. Players work hard to serve three short serves (2-3-4 serving zones), followed by three deep serves (1-6-5 serving zones).

Variations: The coach can vary the serving zone calls, calling for two deep and one short, for example.

Requirements: Six or more players, a coach, two carts of balls and a full court

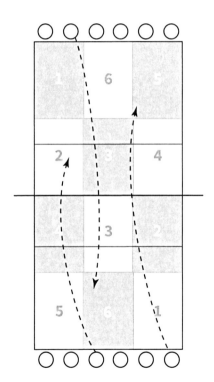

Serving
Touchdown Serves

Difficulty: ● ○ ○

How it works: Players work hard as individuals or small teams to score a football field goal. A coach tapes large uprights, depending on age or challenge level wanted, on the wall for players to serve with accuracy. Remember, coaches, to get those uprights high.

Requirements: Six or more players, uprights taped onto wall, a coach, one ball per player and a full court

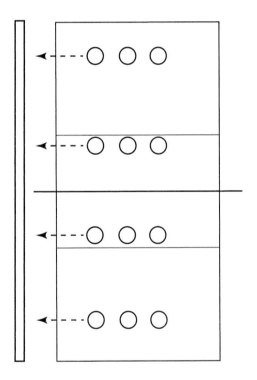

Serving
Water Break Drill

Difficulty: ● ● ●

How it works: Start with three servers on one side, each with a ball. Their partners on the other side start without a ball. Players with a ball attempt to land their serves just past the 10-foot (3 m) line so that it bounces twice before leaving the court. The key is to serve the ball with a low trajectory so it flies under antenna height. Partners retrieve the balls and serve them back, attempting to also serve a "two bouncer." If a service error occurs, both players in the pair sprint toward the other side and switch places. The goal is for all six players to earn 3 points collectively.

Variations: Challenge players to serve a ball that hits the tape then goes over or any other serves you want to work on.

Requirements: Six players, three balls and a full court

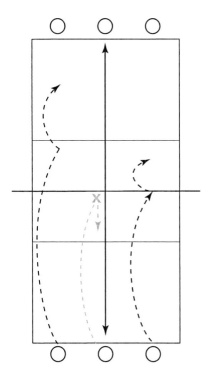

Serving
Won It, Lost It, Tied It

Difficulty: ● ● ○

How it works: The score is 23-24 and your team is down. Players, half on each baseline, are asked to serve two balls. Players complete their serving routine and serve one ball, then the next. If players make both serves, they "won it." If they make only one, they "tied it." If they miss both serves, they "lost it." Players call out the outcome of their serves and go right into the next two serves.

Requirements: Six or more players, a coach, a cart of balls and a full court

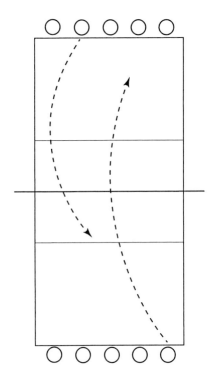

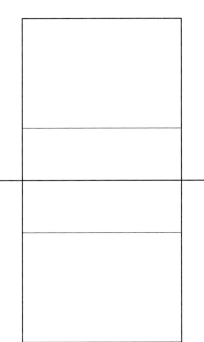

Passing Drills

Passing
Chair Passing

Difficulty: ● ● ○

How it works: In this three-player drill, players are positioned with the tosser in the middle, facing the passer, and the setter or target with his or her back on the net. On a coach's whistle, the ball is slapped and tossed to the passer. The passer then passes the ball all the way up to the setter or target. The setter simply catches the ball on his or her forehead in the setter's window and gently tosses it back to the tosser. On the coach's call, the players rotate: tosser goes to passer, then passer goes to target, and the target becomes the tosser.

Requirements: Three players, a coach, a cart of balls and a half court

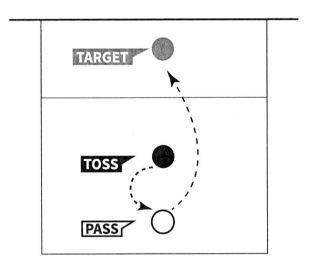

Passing
Fill the Void

Difficulty: ● ● ●

How it works: Half the team is on one side of the net in three lines on the baseline, and the other half of the team mirror that formation. The coach tosses from the same side of the net in this drill. From a toss, players focus on claiming the ball, receiving and passing it, while the nearest player "fills the void." Filling the void means two players pass as one player moves forward to the setter's zone. As the third hit goes over the net, the other side plays out the ball with the right back player also filling the void by running to the setter's zone. Once there's a dead ball or several attempts, players rotate, staying on their side of the net. Showing this in slow motion may help players understand passing to a zone and not each other.

Requirements: Six to 12 players, a coach, a cart of balls and a full court

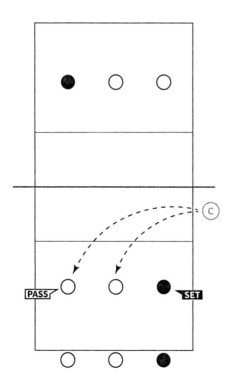

www.theartofcoachingvolleyball.com/youthdb1   **47**

Passing
Four Corners

Difficulty: ● ● ●

How it works: Players divide up equally into four groups, then assemble in lines in a box formation. Instruct players to pass using a cross, line, cross, line pattern. From a coach's toss, the ball travels across the court to the first player in the diagonal, or "cross," line. That player passes back across to the first player in the "line" line. The coach can direct players go to the end of their lines or follow their passes and go to the end of those lines.

Requirements: Eight or more players, a coach, a cart of balls and a half court

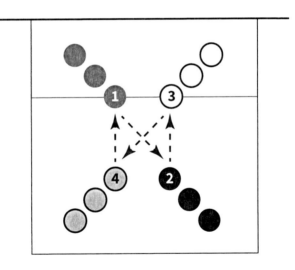

Passing
Four Player Pass and Switch

Difficulty: ●●●

How it works: Players are put in groups of four in a box formation with players facing one another. One player starts the drill by tossing directly to the player across from them. After the toss, the partners next to one another switch. The ball always travels on the same path (1 to 3). The player receiving the toss passes back across to where the toss came from. Players essentially pass to the partner across from them and switch with the one beside them.

Requirements: Four or more players, one ball per group, and a half court

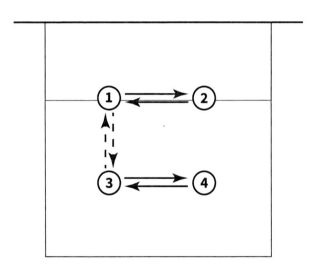

Passing
Free Ball 1,2,3 Drill

Difficulty: ● ○ ○

How it works: As three players at a time enter the floor, the coach tosses a second hit ball. The trio works hard to aggressively send a high and deep free ball over the net. To do this, players pivot and turn a shoulder perpendicular to the net. After playing the ball, players shag or return to their lines. Players in line replace one another as passers abandon their positions.

Variations: A points system divides the floor to emphasize the highest number of points awarded for the deepest free balls. Then challenge your team to earn 20 points.

Requirements: Six or more players, a coach, a cart of balls and a full court

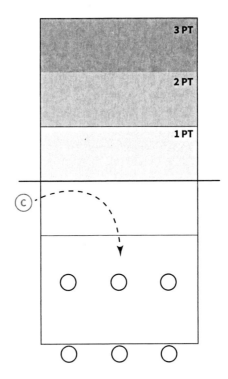

Passing
Free Ball Footwork Drill

Difficulty: ● ● ○

How it works: One player starts in left front at the 10-foot (3 m) line. A second player starts in the setter's position to be the target (T). From the other side of the court, a coach tosses a ball over the net. As this happens, the defensive player makes a step-drop move and prepares to pass. She then chases down the ball and passes it to the target. After the play, the defensive player rotates into the target position and the target person gets in line to pass.

Variations: For a greater challenge, require the team to complete five good passes.

Requirements: Three or more players, a coach, a cart of balls and a full court

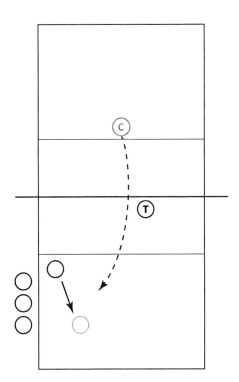

Passing
Handle the Heat Drill

Difficulty: ● ● ○

How it works: Position a large box in the setter's position as a target. On the endline, players assemble in three lines. The first player in each line enters the court, assumes a back row position, and prepares to pass. From across the net, a coach sends a tough serve at the players. Players do their best to handle the serve, working to pass it to the target. After a player passes, they go to the end of the line and are replaced by a new player. The drill repeats until all players have run through the drill several times.

Requirements: Six or more players, a large box, a coach, a cart of balls and a full court

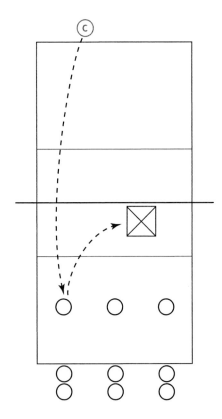

Passing
Hips to the Ball

Difficulty: ● ○ ○

How it works: Players are placed into groups of three with one passer, two tossers and one ball. The tossers' job is to roll the ball back and forth in a straight line. As the tossers roll the ball, the passer shuffles using one or two shuffles or a shuffle-hop to get frozen prior to the ball reaching his or her stance. The ball travels through the passer's feet and they continue shuffling. Coaches call out when they want players to switch.

Requirements: Three or more players in groups of three, one ball per group and a half court

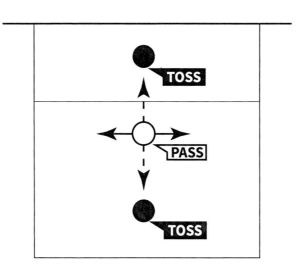

Passing
One-Knee Passing Drill

Difficulty: ● ○ ○

How it works: Players line up single file at the 10-foot (3 m) line. The first player in line goes down on one knee and prepares to pass. One player or a coach stands at the net and tosses a ball at the kneeling player who must pass the ball back from a stationary position.

Variations: Make the drill competitive by requiring players to call the ball or pass the ball high enough for the tosser to catch the ball. The winning group is the one with the most successful completions.

Requirements: Six to 12 players, a cart of balls and a half court

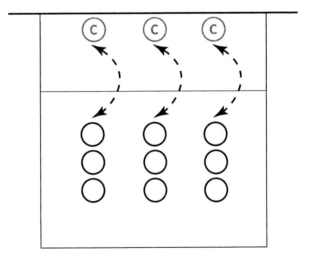

Passing
Partner Ball Rolls

Difficulty: ● ○ ○

How it works: Partners pair up and stand about 10 feet away from each other. Both players squat down and roll a volleyball back and forth. To progress, one player rolls the ball outside the other player's body so they have to shuffle to get to the ball. After several reps, swap roles so both players get a chance to practice their footwork.

Requirements: Two players, one ball and about 10 feet (3 m) of court space

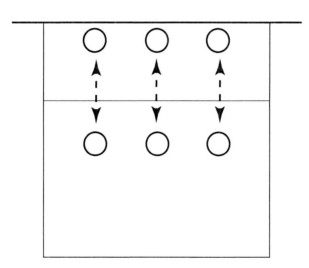

Passing
Partner Pass and Set Drill

Difficulty: ● ● ○

How it works: Instruct players to partner up with one at the net and the other at the 10-foot (3 m) line. The player at the net tosses a short ball to her partner who catches it and sets it back. Next, the tosser lobs a deep ball. To play it, the partner backpedals, passes the ball back and returns to the starting position. Repeat then swap roles after several reps.

Requirements: Two players, one ball and 20 feet of court space

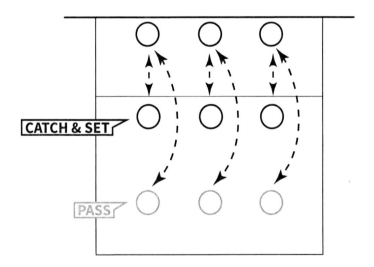

Passing
Partner Passing

Difficulty: ● ● ○

How it works: Players partner up with one at the net and the other about 15 feet away. The player at the net tosses the ball underhand to the player who passes it back. After 10 reps, swap roles.

Variations: To practice movement, have the tosser alternate between short and deep lobs so the passer has to move to play the ball.

Requirements: Two players, one ball and 20 feet of court space

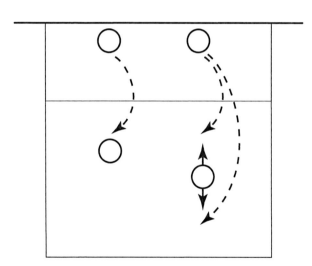

www.theartofcoachingvolleyball.com/youthdb1

Passing
Pass and Switch Drill

Difficulty: ● ● ●

How it works: The coach arranges players in groups of three with one tosser and two passers. The tosser has their back on the net. The tosser tosses the same course with each and every toss. The two passers are side by side. The first passer passes back to the tosser and both passers quickly "Switch, switch, switch!" The passer who passes the ball back to the tosser claims the volleyball by saying, "My ball, my ball!" and the non-passer opens up and says, "Go, go, go!" The coach calls out "New tosser!" to rotate players. Keeping players in the drill for 30-45 seconds will place emphasis on being a low and ready passer. In this drill, all players talk and communicate.

Requirements: Three or more players, a coach, one ball per group and a half court

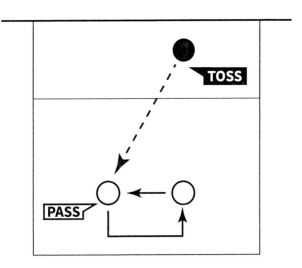

Passing
Pass and Turn Drill

Difficulty: ● ○ ○

How it works: Break into groups of three. Players form a line with 5 feet of space between each player. The two players on the outside each start with a volleyball; the player on the inside does not. Play begins when a player on the outside tosses a ball to the inside passer. They pass the ball back to the tosser before turning to receive a ball from the other outside player. The inside passer then turns again to receive a ball from the first tosser. Repeat this pattern for several reps, then swap the inside player for one of the outsides until all players have had a chance to pass.

Requirements: Three players, two balls and 10 feet of court space

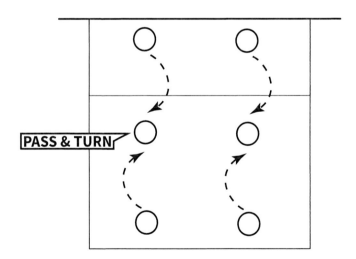

Passing
Passing Footwork on Command

Difficulty: ● ○ ○

How it works: Players spread out in a half court space and assume a low, ready position. A coach stands at the net and directs players to shuffle right, left, backward or forward using hand signals. When the coach makes a fist, players stop and shout, "I go!" and execute a pass without a ball. The goal is for players to stay low as they shuffle.

Requirements: Six to 12 players, a coach and a half court

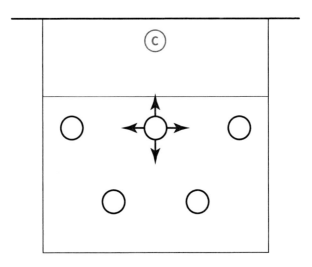

Passing
Pretzel Drill

Difficulty: ● ● ○

How it works: This drill has players in groups of four. There's a tosser with his or her back on the net and three passers about 15 feet (4.5 m) out in front of the tosser. Moving in the shape of a "pretzel," players pass and switch with the player immediately next to them. The tosser switches up who gets the toss. If the ball is tossed to the middle passer, outside players must hold for a split-second as the middle passer picks who to switch with. The pretzel-like movement continues until the coach switches players. This control passing drill can be timed for 30-45 seconds.

Requirements: Four or more players, a coach, a ball and a half court

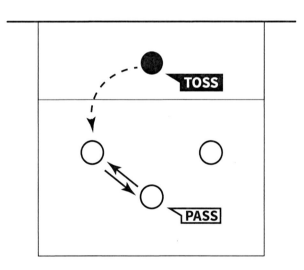

Passing
Queen of the Throne

Difficulty: ● ● ●

How it works: A chair is set out on the floor, close to the net where the Queen (Q) can sit on her throne! The Queen has a Peasant (P) working next to her. The Peasant is the royal tosser. The Peasant tosses to the three Princesses (PR); they are the passers who want to be the Queen. The sportsmanlike component to the challenge is that the Queen must try to catch a pass, but she cannot come off her throne. Once a Princess's ball has been caught, she replaces the old Queen so that now there's a new queen.

Variations: Every 1 or 2 minutes, the coach can call out for a new tosser. An extra player is the Joker (J) who shags and keeps a ball in the Peasant's hand.

Requirements: Six or more players, a chair or box, a coach, a cart of balls and a full court

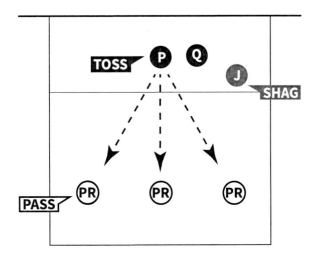

Passing
Run-Through Drill

Difficulty: ● ● ○

How it works: Players line up single file in left back with a coach in the setter's position at the net. The first player starts in ready position. The coach lobs the ball and the player chases it down, plays the pass and runs through the space. Players need to keep their bottoms down as they run, so they can get under the ball and pop it up to the target (T).

Requirements: Six to 12 players, a coach, a cart of balls and a half court

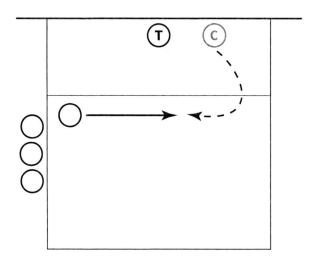

Passing
Serve Receive Wave Drill

Difficulty: ● ● ●

How it works: Set up with three passers (P), three servers (S) and a target (T) on each side of the net. At the same time, one server on each side serves to the opposite team. Passers then pass the ball to the target who is at the net. Teams earn a point for every pass the target can catch without moving more than one step. After every three points earned, servers rotate to a new serving location on their same side and passers do the same. Once the combined score of both teams reaches 10 points, servers on side 1 become passers on side 1. Passers on side 1 become passers on side 2. Passers on side 2 become servers on side 2. Servers on side 2 become servers on side 1. Play continues as before.

Variations: For more experienced players, take the score back to zero for every overpass or dead ball.

Requirements: Twelve players, two coaches or targets, two carts of balls and a full court

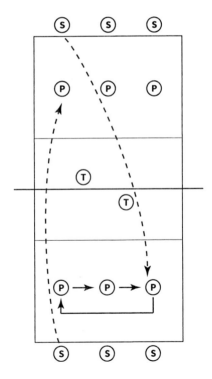

Passing
Shuffle Back Passing

Difficulty: ● ● ○

How it works: Players partner up with one player holding the ball. Both players start with their backs on the net. On the ball slap, the passing partner turns and backpedals to receive the toss from his or her partner. The first toss is short, just behind the 10-foot (3 m) line. Once the first pass is completed, the passer backpedals to the longer distance on the baseline. Passers work to shuffle low and athletically, then hop and freeze to pass the ball.

Variations: Passers learn to drop, cross and hop-hop to get their feet set and frozen to deliver the pass.

Requirements: Two or more players, one ball per pair and a half court

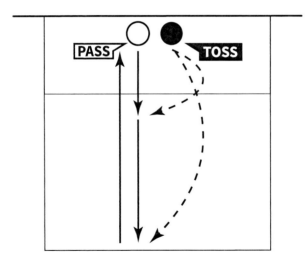

Passing
Shuffle, Shuffle, Freeze Dance

Difficulty: ● ○ ○

How it works: Players are positioned in a group formation in lines with plenty of room. Like a team dance, players follow the coach's lead and call out the footwork. Players move together in a rhythm going 6-8 different directions. The coach can define the directions prior to beginning. Players must stay low and get through the 6-8 spots and recover back to the middle each time. Remember, coaches, to face the net or have your back to the players so they can truly mirror your moves.

Variations: Add a simulated movement of passing or setting at the completion of each footwork pattern.

Requirements: Six or more players, a coach and a half court

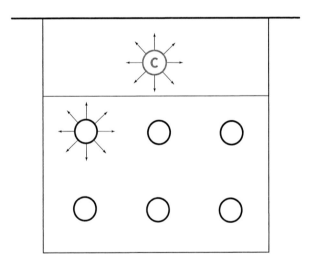

Passing
Step-Hop Drill

Difficulty: ● ● ○

How it works: Two players stand side-by-side at the net. The passing partner stands to the partner's right and faces the net. The tossing partner faces away from the net.

1. The passer backpedals to the 10-foot (3 m) line.
2. Then takes a step-hop to the left. The tosser lobs a ball to the passer who passes it back.
3. The passer returns to their partner at the net, this time going to the left side.

The passer then repeats the process by backpedaling to the 10-foot line again, taking a step-hop to the right before passing the ball back to the tosser and running to the net on the partners right side. Repeat the pattern for a designated number of reps.

Requirements: Two players, one ball and about 20 feet of court space

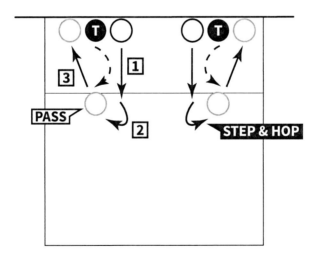

Passing
Target Spots

Difficulty: ● ● ○

How it works: The target spots are either large free ball areas (FB) across the net from the players or a designated setter's zone (SZ) on the same side of the net. With two lines of passers and a coach in middle front tossing, the coach can either call out a zone or have players attempt a controlled pass to zone or an aggressive free ball to the large area across the net.

Note: players should have two different looks as they adjust to the ball or skill; hips to the ball, frozen passing or a free-ball stance, hips to the sideline with their shoulder closest to the net dropped for an aggressive free ball.

Requirements: Four or more players, a coach, a cart of balls and a full court

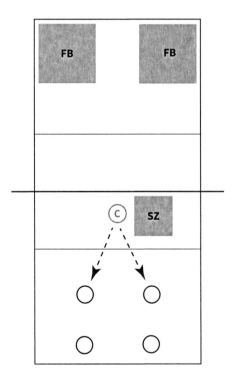

Passing
Team Popcorn Drill

Difficulty: ●●○

How it works: This communication drill trains all players to stay disciplined to a specific area or zone on the floor. The entire team is on one side of the net. The coach is positioned on the other side of the net. Coach quickly puts up one toss after another over the net as players communicate, identify, claim and pass the volleyball to the setter's zone. The goal might be reaching a designated number of consecutive touches or keeping the ball from hitting the floor for 30 seconds (timed).

Requirements: Six or more players, a coach, a cart of balls and a full court

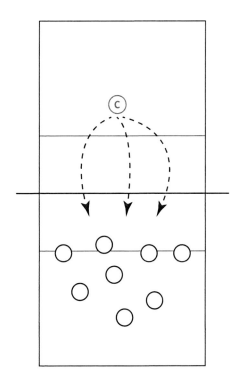

Passing
Three-Man Passing

Difficulty: ● ● ○

How it works: Break into groups of five players, each group taking ⅓ of the court and a ball. Three passers start at the 10-foot (3 m) line, one catcher stands at the net, and the tosser stands in the front row on the opposite side of the net. The tosser lobs a ball over the net to the first passer in line, who then passes it to the catcher at the net. The catcher returns the ball to the tosser. The drill repeats with each passer taking a turn.

Variations: After the initial pass, the catcher sets back to the passer, and the passer passes the ball over the net to the tosser.

Requirements: Five players, a ball and a full court

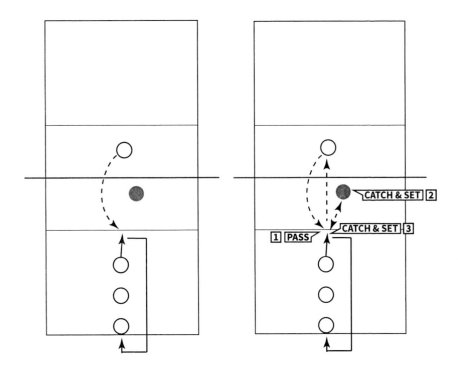

Passing
Toss, Claim, Catch Drill

Difficulty: ● ○ ○

How it works: Players have a partner across the net. After slapping the ball, the tosser throws the ball over the net. The receiver shuffles to get their hips to the ball and catches it in a low position. The receiveing player then stands up and bounce the ball to the tosser and gets ready to move again.

Requirements: Two or more players, one ball per pair and a full court

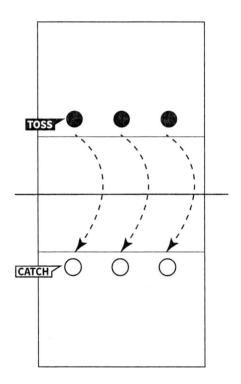

www.theartofcoachingvolleyball.com/youthdb1

Passing
Wall Touch Passing

Difficulty: ● ● ○

How it works: The passing partner starts with their back on the wall while the tossing partner is about 12-20 feet from the wall. The passer's challenge is to drop step and open their hips to shuffle back to the wall, touch it, and return to the passing ready position. The passer then control passes back to the tosser. The tosser must wait for the passer to touch the wall before slapping the ball with an "It's up!" call. The coach rotates players every 45 seconds to a minute. Challenge the passer to not stand up between passing but stay low the entire time.

Requirements: Two or more players, a wall, a coach, one ball per pair and about 20 feet of space

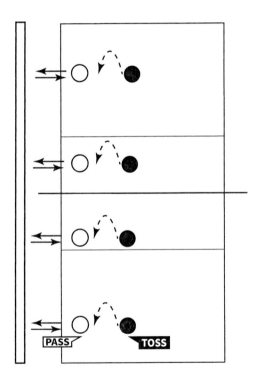

Setting Drills

Setting
Basketball Keys Drill

Difficulty: ● ● ○

How it works: This partner drill teaches setters to cover the court quickly using four different movement patterns: shuffle, run, outside plant and inside spin.

Begin with a coach in middle back and the setter at the net in zone 3. The coach lobs balls in a semi-circle formation, alternating between on and off the net positions, for the setter to return. The setter moves back and forth between the two points using these four movement patterns:

- Shuffle
- Run
- Outside plant
- Inside spin

The setter performs each movement 10 times before moving on to the next one.

Requirements: One player, a coach, a cart of balls and a half court

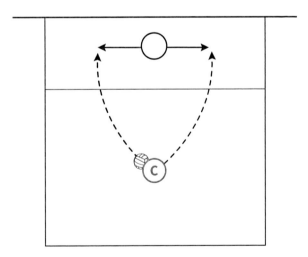

Setting
Beginner Setting Drills

Difficulty: ● ○ ○

How it works: These drills work well for young players or older players who need practice setting.

- **Drill 1:** Partners line up about 10 feet (3 m) apart. Each pair starts with two balls. Player 1 rolls the first ball on the ground to player 2 as player 2 sets the second ball to player 1.
- **Drill 2:** Two players sit across from each other with the soles of their shoes touching. Using only one ball, the players set back and forth from their sitting positions.

Variations:
- Drill 1:
  - **Variation 1:** Player 1 bounces the first ball to player 2 as player 2 sets the second ball to player 1.
  - **Variation 2:** Player 1 kicks the first ball to player 2 as player 2 sets the second ball to player 1.

Requirements: Two or more players, two balls per pair and a half court

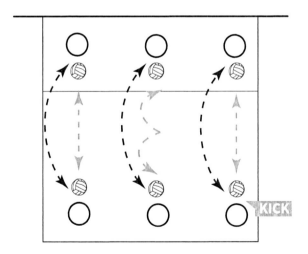

www.theartofcoachingvolleyball.com/youthdb1

Setting
Ground Setting Drill

Difficulty: ● ○ ○

How it works: Begin with one player sitting cross-legged on the floor. From about 10 feet (3 m) away, the tosser tosses the ball to the setter. The setting player catches the ball high above their head, using the proper "triangle" hand work. Then they release the ball and send it back to the tosser.

Variations: The next step is to have players set the ball back with no catch in between.

Requirements: Two players, a ball and 10 feet of court space

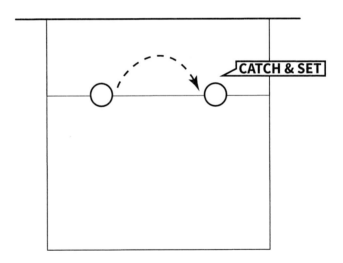

Setting
Half-Star Setting Drill

Difficulty: ● ● ●

How it works: Set up on a half court with a setter in zone 3 and a coach in zone 6. The coach lobs three consecutive balls for the setter to set toward the pin: the first at the net's middle, the second at 45 degrees off the net, and a third at 90 degrees off the net. The setter moves toward the ball, squares up, sets to the outside pin, then returns to her starting position. This series repeats twice for a total of six balls.

Variations: Repeat the drill with the setter making back sets. Additionally, you may want to simplify the drill and focus on one thing at a time, such as weight transfer, getting square to the outside consistently, or finishing to the target.

Requirements: One player, a coach, a cart of balls and a half court

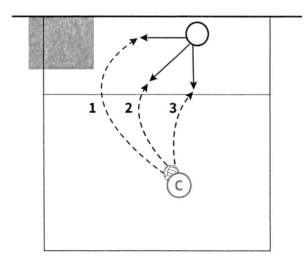

Setting
Partner Knee Work

Difficulty: ● ● ○

How it works: This partner drill sets up with one player on their knees. The second player tosses the ball from about 10 feet away. The player sets the ball back to the tosser using good setting form.

Variations: After completing a series of forward sets, switch to back sets. Add a third player to catch the back sets and return the ball to the tosser.

Requirements: Two to three players, a ball and 10 feet of court space

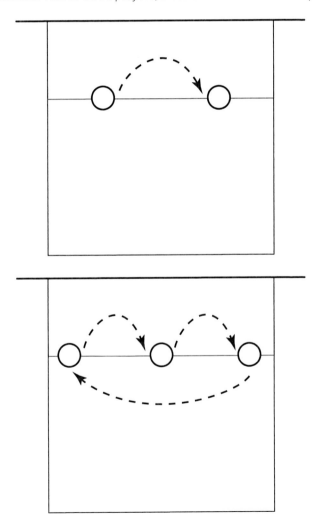

Setting
Partner Setting Drill

Difficulty: ● ○ ○

How it works: Players have a partner and are positioned on the floor across from one another. The tosser tosses from the baseline toward the net to the setter. The setter receives or catches the ball as she faces the tosser, then proceeds to turn her right shoulder toward the net. Setters practice drawing theirs hands from the middle of their body up to the "setter's window." "Circle your belly-button" is a way to remind players how and where to rest their hands as they move to get to the ball. Setters can progress to a full set, in time.

Requirements: Six or more players, a cart of balls and a half court

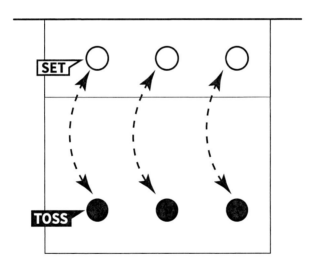

Setting
Rapid Fire Setting

Difficulty: ● ● ○

How it works: Players set up like they are beginning a partner drill with one partner backed up against the net and the other a fews steps in front of the baseline. The players at the net are the tossers and the players near the baseline are the setters. All the tossers slap the ball and give an "It's up!" call on the coach's whistle. The setters then set the ball back to the tosser. Then, all the setters rotate one position before the next toss. Remember to switch up your tossers and setters so all players get their setting touches.

Variations: Speed up the drill and make the players move faster.

Requirements: Six or more players, a coach, one ball per pair and a half court

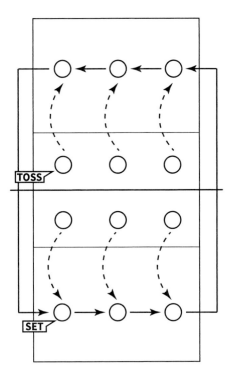

Setting
S5 Target Sets

Difficulty: ●●●

How it works: In this drill, all players are setters. Begin with three setters in the back row and two setters in the front row. The coach tosses or sends a free ball to the back row setters. The three back row setters (S1, S2, S3) set to S4, who is positioned in the setter's zone. S4 sets to S5, who is positioned in the Outside Hitter position. S5 shoot sets the volleyball over the net.

Requirements: Five players, a coach, a cart of balls and a full court

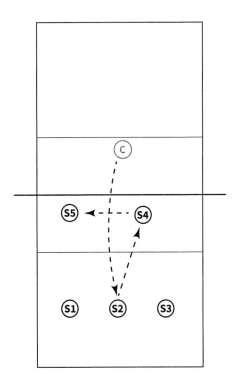

www.theartofcoachingvolleyball.com/youthdb1

Setting
Setter Training Progression

Difficulty: ● ● ○

How it works: To begin this progression drill, players pair up and grab one ball per group.

- **Progression 1:** Player 1 bounces a ball to player 2 who sits on the ground about 5 feet away. Player 2 holds the ball at her forehead, then fires it back to her partner.
- **Progression 2:** Player 1 bounces a ball to player 2 who sits on the ground about 5 feet away. Player 2 tosses the ball to herself, then fires it back to her partner.
- **Progression 3:** Both players stand and move to the 10-foot (3 m) line on opposite sides of the net. Player 1 tosses the ball into the air as she steps with her lead foot and sets the ball over the net to her partner using a single or double touch.
- **Progression 4:** Both players stand and move to the 10-foot (3 m) line on opposite sides of the net. Player 1 tosses the ball in front of her, letting it bounce once. As it rebounds, she moves under the ball and sets it over the net to her partner.

Requirements: Two or more players, one ball per group and a full court

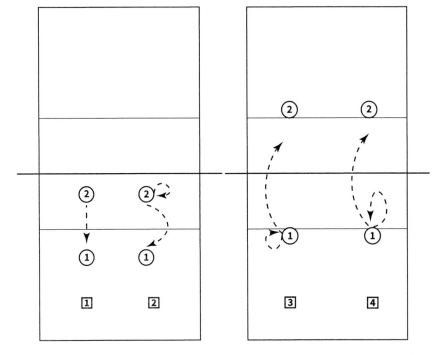

Setting
Setter's Call Drill

Difficulty: ● ● ●

How it works: This drill is designed to help setters identify when they just can't get to a bad pass. The coach makes a toss that is difficult or impossible for the setter to get to, and the setter must shout, "Help! Help! Help!" The alternative setter does his or her best to put the volleyball out in front of a hitter. Hitters must communicate and work to successfully get the third hit over. This drill reminds players that all players need to be ready to set. The coach can rotate players around the floor or wash the drill, making sure all players start in the setting position. The coach reminds players to run with their hands free and to draw their setter's hands once their feet are frozen.

Requirements: Six or more players, a coach, a cart of balls and a half court

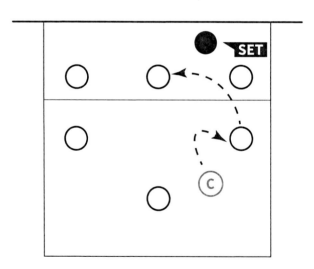

Setting
Setting Fan Drill

Difficulty: ● ● ○

How it works: To set up this drill, position a setter at the net, a target player in left front, a coach behind the 10-foot (3 m) line with a player ready to hand them a ball, and any extra players on the right sideline. The coach tosses to the setter. Using proper hand technique and footwork, the setter sets the ball to the left front catcher. Players then rotate counterclockwise to the next position.

Variations: The coach tosses the ball midway between the setter and left front positions. This requires the setter to run forward to make the set. When working with one setter, start the player at the net, then move her to different positions off the net in a fan shape.

Requirements: Three or more players, a coach, a cart of balls and a half court

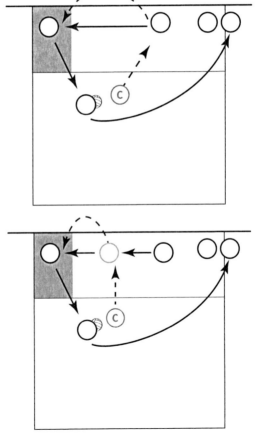

Setting
Setting Lines

Difficulty: ● ● ○

How it works: Start with a group of six with three players per side. Tossers are on one side and setters on the other. Tossers lob an underhand ball to the first setter in line on the opposite side. The setter catches the ball at her forehead, then returns it to the tosser by setting it over the net. The tosser and setter go to the end of the line, and the drill repeats with the next tosser-setter pair.

Variations: More experienced setters can set or jump set without catching the ball.

Requirements: Six players, one ball and a full court

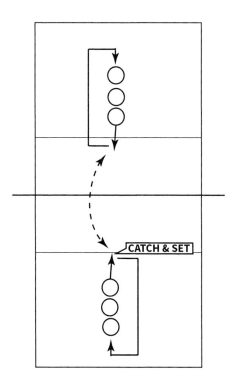

www.theartofcoachingvolleyball.com/youthdb1   89

Setting
Stability Ball Drill

Difficulty: ● ● ○

How it works: This partner exercise offers a greater challenge for players learning proper setting handwork. To begin, player 1 sits on a stability ball. Player 2 tosses a ball from about 10 feet away. Player 1 sets the ball back to player 2 using proper "triangle" hand form while trying to maintain a neutral body position. Be sure to instruct players to stay within their midline and to finish through the bottom of the palms when setting.

Variations: After completing a series of forward sets, switch to back sets.

Requirements: Two players, a stability ball, a volleyball and 10 feet of court space

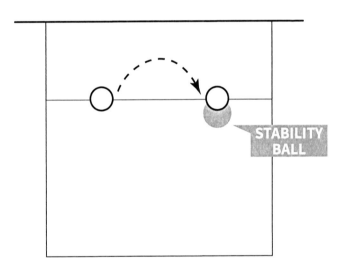

Setting
Star Footwork Patterns

Difficulty: ● ● ●

How it works: This half-court drill sets up with a setter in base position at the net's middle. The coach runs the setter through these six different footwork patterns:

1. Standing in the setting zone.
2. Hop-shuffle step parallel to the net toward the left pin.
3. Two steps away from the net at a 45-degree angle toward the left pin.
4. Two steps at a 90-degree angle off the net.
5. Two steps away from the net at a 45-degree angle toward the right pin.
6. Hop-shuffle step parallel to the net toward the right pin.

After running each route, the setter returns to base in ready position with knees loaded and face toward the court. Repeat each of the six patterns twice.

Variations: Once a setter has the footwork down, add a ball and do triangle setting. Use short antenna work with younger players instead of long, reverse flow.

Requirements: One player, a coach and a half court

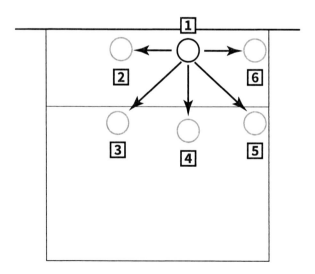

Setting
Target Setting

Difficulty: ● ● ●

How it works: Six "targets" or players set up in areas the coach designates. Setters line up in right back, ready to hustle to the setting zone. Once the setter gets to the net, he or she moves left. Before tossing a ball to the setter, the coach calls out the target and the setter sets to that area. The setter then shags the ball and returns to the line as a new setter rotates onto the court. The coach emphasizes the right foot slightly forward and the weight transfer out to that front leg as the setter lengthens and extends.

Variations: Instead of setting to just one area, have setters set to all six.

Requirements: Three or more players, a coach, a cart of balls and a half court

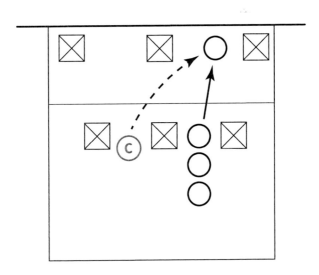

Check out the youth drill videos we have online!

Setting
Tennis Ball Setting

Difficulty: ● ○ ○

How it works: Players partner up and position themselves with one player at the net and the other at the 10-foot (3 m) line. Player 1 tosses a tennis ball to her partner using a two-hand, underhand technique, ending with hands raised above her head for a target. Player 2 returns the ball using the same motion.

Instruct players to catch the ball with their hands above their heads and elbows slightly out and level with their shoulders. Their thumbs should angle toward their cheek bones, and their hands should wrap around the ball, but not touch the back or sides of it. Players need to focus on the ball and move quickly, getting their bodies directly behind the ball. They also need to follow through like Supergirl, holding this position until their partners catch the ball.

Variations: For practice with deep setting, movement and positioning, try the "short and deep" variation. Player 2 backpedals from the 10-foot (3 m) line to the back court as player 1 tosses the tennis ball. Player 2 executes a deep catch and set technique, then returns to the 10-foot (3 m) line for the short catch and set. Alternate short and deep tosses for several reps, then swap positions so player 1 gets a turn.

Requirements: Six players, one tennis ball per pair and a half court

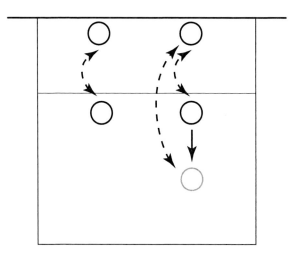

Setting
Triangle Hand Placement Drill

Difficulty: ● ○ ○

How it works: This simple drill teaches proper handwork to setters. To begin, players place their hands in a triangle shape on the ball. They spread their fingers wide and wraps them around the ball in a circular shape. Keeping proper hand form, the player raises the ball above their head above their hairline. Arms are extended and elbows bent with no other movement in the arms. After a moment, the player returns to the starting position while maintaining a proper hold on the ball. Repeat this up and down movement several times to get a feel for the proper hand position.

Requirements: One player, a coach, and a ball

95

Attacking Drills

Attacking
Alligator Attacks

Difficulty: ● ● ○

How it works: Players are positioned in a line, angled to hit. Two jump ropes act as the alligator in the drill, so that the alligator is directly in the 45° attack of the hitter. Players learn to jump over the alligator with a distinct step-close. The first step in our three-step hitting approach is behind the alligator, and jumping over the alligator is the step-close. Players then jump and land before heading to the back of the line for another attempt.

Variations: The coach can add a controlled toss once over the alligator for the players to get the feeling of jumping and contacting the ball.

Requirements: One or more players, a coach, a cart of balls and a full court

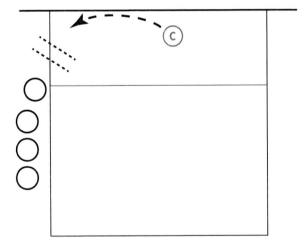

Attacking
Box Hitting Drill

Difficulty: ● ○ ○

How it works: Set up a box at the net on the left side. Players line up behind the box. One at a time, players step onto the box and hit two consecutive balls the coach tosses to them. The focus is on using a draw-whip-snap motion. Once players master the box hit, they may progress to hitting from a standing position (no jumping) on the floor.

Variations: Make the drill into a game with two teams competing to see who can get a designated number of hits over the net first. Run the game with or without the box.

Requirements: Two or more players, one box, a coach, a cart of balls and a full court

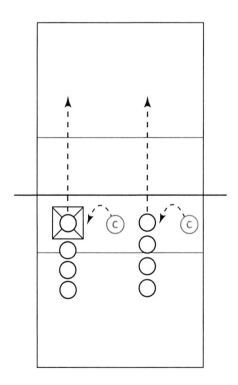

Attacking
Hitting Jail Break

Difficulty: ● ● ○

How it works: The game Jailbreak typically has all players serving, but in this version players hit off the coach's toss. Players that successfully hit the ball over the net return to the back of the hitting line and keep hitting, but a player who misses a hit must go to "jail" on the other side of the net. In jail, hitters become diggers. To get out of jail and back into the hitting line, a player claims and digs the volleyball. The player whose ball was dug switches with the digger and goes to jail. The way to win the game is to be the last hitter swinging and get a kill against all teammates trying to dig you.

Variations: At random times, the coach yells, "Jailbreak!" This clears out the jail and frees all the players to become hitters.

Requirements: Four or more players, a coach, a cart of balls and a full court

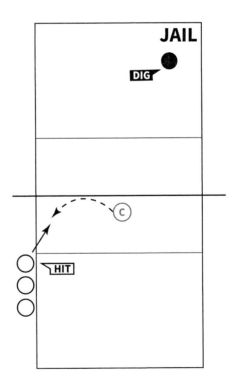

Attacking
Net Down Balls Drill

Difficulty: ● ● ○

How it works: Partners face one another, each standing on their respective 10-foot (3 m) line. Start a full step in toward the net and begin hitting down balls so that the ball bounces once under the net to the other partner. Players back up on cue from the coach. Players are learning where and how to strike the ball to adjust its rebound.

Variations: More advanced players can attempt to put topspin on the hits.

Requirements: Two or more players, a coach, one ball per pair and a full court

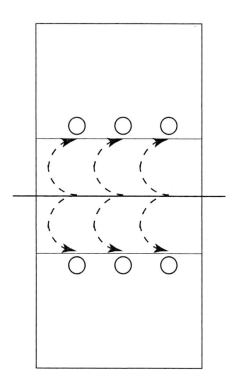

www.theartofcoachingvolleyball.com/youthdb1   103

Attacking
Red, White, and Blue Hitting Drill

Difficulty: ● ● ○

How it works: This basic striking drill focuses on ball alignment on the hitting shoulder and learning to hit with an open hand. Players must ask for the ball by yelling, "Red, red, red!," "White, white, white!" or "Blue, blue, blue!" Once the coach hears them calling for the ball, the coach tosses a high toss. Players shuffle to get their shoulder lined up with the ball, point with their off-hand to the ball (track), and get into the trophy top pose. Stepping with the opposite foot and smacking the ball should be complete with a "firm finish," and the statue pose at the end where the player is not falling off balance after contact.

Requirements: Three or more players, a coach, a cart of balls and a full court

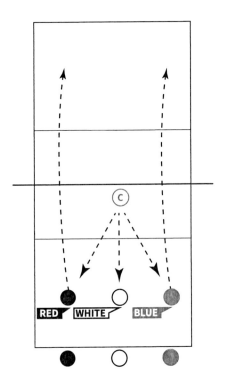

Attacking
Reds and Outsides Hitting

Difficulty: ● ● ○

How it works: The team is divided into two equal hitting lines. The outside attackers (O) are lined up near the 10-foot (3 m) line outside of the court. Positioned not far behind them and inside the floor are the back row attackers (R). The outside hitters are calling out "4, 4, 4!" The back row attackers are calling out "Red, red, red!" The name of these attacking positions vary from state to state, by program and by coach. Hitters hit the outside or the back row attack and dip under the net to shag, then return to the hitting lines.

Requirements: Two or more players, a coach, a cart of balls and a full court

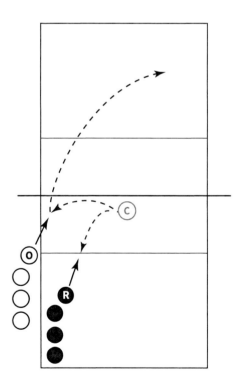

www.theartofcoachingvolleyball.com/youthdb1   **105**

Attacking
Team Hitting Drill

Difficulty: ● ● ○

How it works: Players line up in three lines behind the 10-foot (3m) line and one by one, step up to hit, tip, or shoot set over the net. Players hit one and dip under the net to shag after the contact. A team goal of 10 tips, 10 hits and 10 shoot sets add up to 30 successful hits or the goal could be as simple as 10 total of any of the front row attacks.

Variations: The coach may call out which specific attack they want from a player.

Requirements: Three or more players, a coach, a cart of balls and a full court

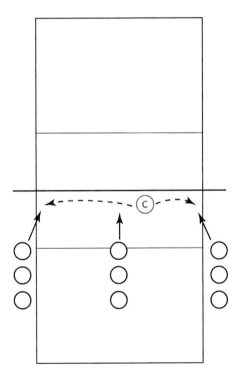

Attacking
Three Hits Goal

Difficulty: ● ● ○

How it works: Outside, middle, and right side hitters line up in three lines behind the 10-foot (3m) line ready to jump and swing. The coach sets a goal for the team, for example, 10 good swings. From a coach's toss, players take a full approach, jump and hit. The coach may also challenge the three hitters by asking for a particular hit: tip, off-speed, line shot, cross-court shot, deep corner, etc. When the individual hitter is successful with the coach's call, they add a point to the team goal.

Requirements: Three or more players, a coach, a cart of balls and a full court

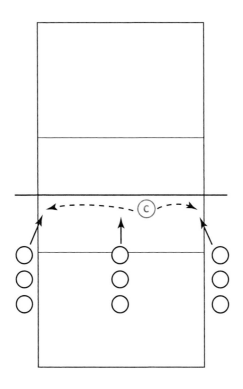

Attacking
Wall Spiking Drill

Difficulty: ● ○ ○

How it works: Have players stand about 10-15 feet from a wall or garage door. Players then toss the ball into the air, spot the ball (with the non-hitting hand), reach up high, rotate the upper body and hit the ball downward toward a spot on the ground. The ball should then bounce towards the wall and back to the player. Repeat.

Requirements: One player, a wall and a ball

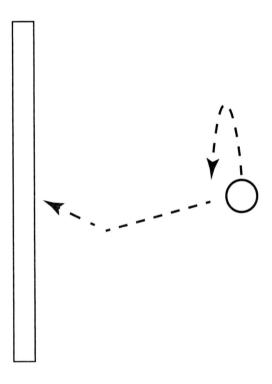

Defense Drills

Defense
Blocker Wall

Difficulty: ● ● ●

How it works: The coach steps in as the outside hitter and has five other players around them to cover the hit. The coach then swings or throws the ball into the blocking wall (a football blocking pad works well) and the hit deflects off the block. Players dig the ball out of hitter coverage and play it out. Players are reminded to talk and transition quickly to offense.

Variations: If players are more skilled, add an outside hitter who hits into the block from a set that can come from a coach's toss or the setter.

Requirements: Five to six players, a blocking device, a coach, a cart of balls and a full court

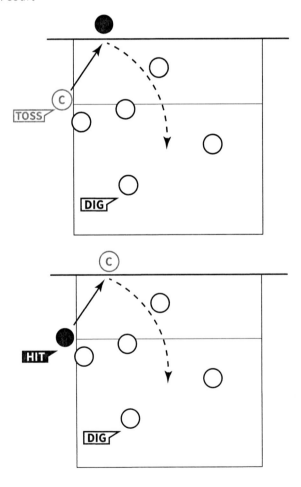

Check out the youth drill videos we have online!

Defense
Bounce and Chase Drill

Difficulty: ● ● ○

How it works: Players line up about 25 feet away from the coach. The first player in line starts in ready position. The coach tosses a ball somewhere near the player—or not so near—and the player must sprint and catch the ball before it bounces twice. The key is for the player to get faster as she gets closer to the ball.

Requirements: Three or more players, a coach, a cart of balls and a half court

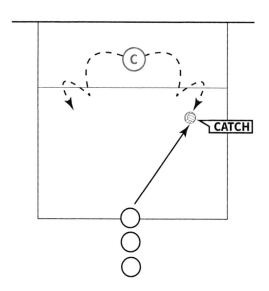

www.theartofcoachingvolleyball.com/youthdb1   **115**

Defense
Chase Drill

Difficulty: ● ● ○

How it works: Two players start at the net. A coach standing at the net on the other side lobs a ball to a hard-to-reach place on the court. Both players must chase it down and cooperatively play it back over the net. The drill repeats with the next two players.

Requirements: Two or more players, a coach, a cart of balls and a full court

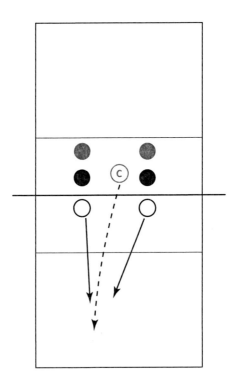

Defense
Cone Agility Drill

Difficulty: ● ○ ○

How it works: A coach places a marker on the floor (blue painter's tape works well) with four marks or cones in a cross shape around the middle marker The distance from the center marker to the outside marks is 6 feet. One player starts at the center marker and the coach times that person's agility effort as he or she extends from one mark to the next, four touches total.

Players start at the center marker and move toward the right marker, touch the mark, and return to the center marker. Next, the player heads forward to the front mark, then left. Lastly, to complete the course the player must touch the final mark, back. To stop the clock, the player must go back to the center marker, so that the player ends where he or she began.

Variations: A coach or partner can add tosses at the marks for the player to pass.

Requirements: One or more players, floor or painter's tape, a coach and a half court

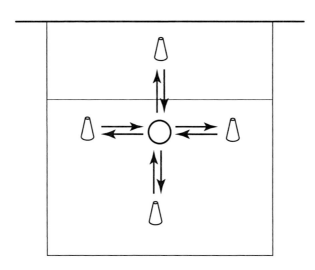

www.theartofcoachingvolleyball.com/youthdb1

Defense
Dig to Boxes

Difficulty: ● ● ○

How it works: Use floor tape to create two small boxes on the court, one at left front and another at right front. Position a player in each box and a coach at middle front who will bounce the ball to simulate a bad first pass.

- **Drill 1:** The remaining players line up at middle back. The defensive player scrambles for the ball and attempts to deliver it high to one of the boxes. The team must make seven good passes before they can move on to the next drill.
- **Drill 2:** The remaining players line up in right and left back. One defensive player handles the first pass and the other player takes the second, attempting to deliver it to one of the boxes at the net. The team must make 10 good passes before moving on to the next drill.

Requirements: Three or more players, floor tape, a coach, a cart of balls and a half court

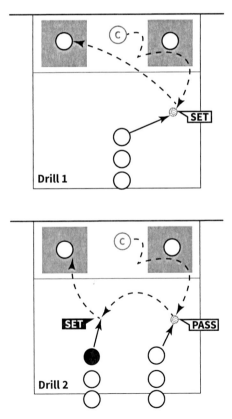

118 Check out the youth drill videos we have online!

Defense
Digging Challenge

Difficulty: ● ● ●

How it works: A formation of three hitters vs. four diggers allows the defense to adjust so that they are able to cover and dig. The coach places four defenders in basic position who must adjust to the three hitters' attacking angles. The coach tosses a ball to the hitters, and the diggers play it out. Players can rotate through on defense and the hitters can also switch hitting positions.

Variations: Rotate diggers after three digs, scoring their performance as follows: a great dig = 3 points, a good dig = 2 points and an overpass = -1. The coach can define the setter's zone using cones, a taped area, or a gym mat.

Requirements: Seven players, cones, tape or a gym mat, a coach, a cart of balls and a full court

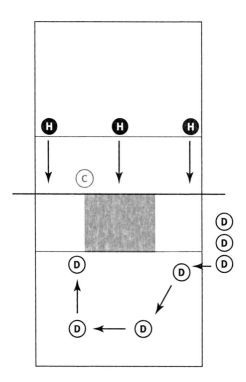

www.theartofcoachingvolleyball.com/youthdb1

Defense
Elastic Digging Drill

Difficulty: ● ● ○

How it works: To set up this drill, run an elastic cord between two poles. This shows players how low they need to be when they dig the ball. Place a cone at each end of the elastic cord.

The drill begins with a player in "monkey" position—feet wide with arms hanging straight down. Starting at the near cone, the first player shuffles backward at an angle toward their right, then digs a down ball from the coach. The player continues to shuffle to the right, moving forward at an angle toward the far cone. After touching the cone, they shuffle backward again at an angle, digs another down ball from the coach and finishes the pattern by shuffling forward toward the near cone. The goal is for players to stay below the elastic guide rope as they shuffle from one point to another.

Requirements: One or more players, two cones, two poles and an elastic band, a coach, a cart of balls and a half court

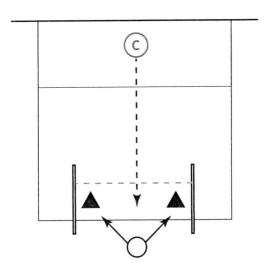

Defense
Knockout Digging Drill

Difficulty: ● ● ○

How it works: To set up this knockout drill, use tape to mark out a small box on the court with a larger box surrounding it. Players line up along the left sideline. A coach standing at the setter's position hits a down ball at the first player in line. That player digs the ball, then tries to catch it. The best dig is one that the player catches in the small box. The second best dig is caught in the bigger box. The third best dig is one that is caught anywhere on the court. The least desirable dig is a ball that's not caught. If the player who follows you in the drill makes a better dig than you do, you're out. The winner is the last player "standing."

Requirements: Three or more players, floor tape, a coach, a cart of balls and a half court

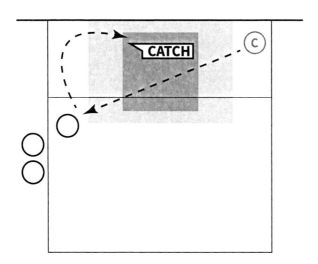

Defense
Step and Stick

Difficulty: ● ○ ○

How it works: This defensive drill has players in two lines facing the coach. The first two players step onto the floor, low and ready to step and stick. The ball contact should be low as the coach can control the intensity of the throw or down ball. The players dig their ball, shag it, and return it to the ball cart before heading back to their digging lines.

Variations: The coach may say, "All digs will be to your right" or "All digs will be to your left" to give players a sense of quick success with less reading or having to guess where the ball with fall.

Requirements: Two or more players, a coach, a cart of balls and a half court

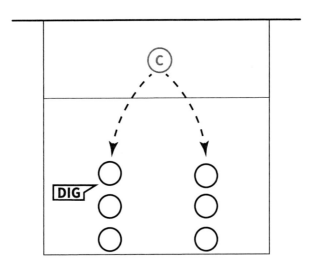

Defense
Ten to Win

Difficulty: ● ● ○

How it works: Players are positioned on one side of the net in defense and the coach puts a ball into play. Defensive players (D) work to dig the ball as the Blockers (B) work to jump and "release" off the net as they land. Once players get 10 digs or ups, they rotate into a new position. Remind defensive players to stay low as they adjust rather than moving tall and then dropping to a low position.

Requirements: Six players, a coach, a cart of balls and a half court

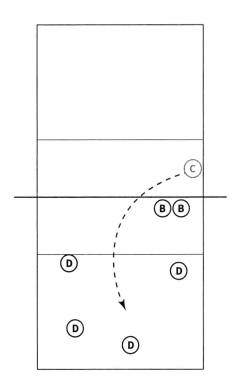

www.theartofcoachingvolleyball.com/youthdb1   123

Defense
Tennis Ball Touch

Difficulty: ● ○ ○

How it works: Either with a coach in middle front or as pairs, players toss a tennis ball towards a defensive player who is trying to reach and touch the ball. Players are encouraged to move toward the tennis ball to get the touch. The coach can count touches or simply let players work to meet the touch challenge. Players switch or rotate every 1-2 minutes on the coach's whistle.

Requirements: Two or more players, a coach, a cart of balls and a half court

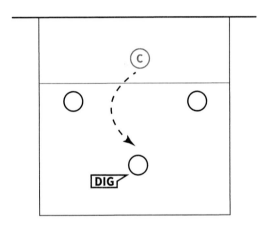

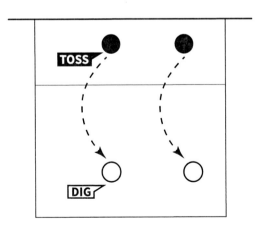

Check out the youth drill videos we have online!

Defense
Toss and Collapse Drill

Difficulty: ● ● ○

How it works: Two players start under the net in a forward-leaning defensive posture with toes behind their shoulders. Remaining players form two lines behind them. A coach tosses a ball in front of the first player in line. The player catches the ball, releases it quickly, collapses to the floor and gets back in line. Players progress to actually digging the ball.

Variations: To work on an offensive approach to defense, have players start under the net, shuffle backward a few steps, then drive forward, play the ball and collapse to the floor.

Requirements: Ten to 12 players, two coaches, two carts of balls and a full court

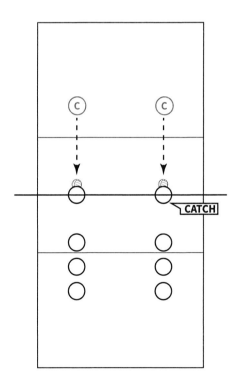

www.theartofcoachingvolleyball.com/youthdb1   125

128

129

Ball Control Drills

Ball Control
1-on-1 Competitive Drill

Difficulty: ● ● ●

How it works: Split the court in half by attaching an antenna to the middle of the net. Position one player on each side of the net. The challenger starts the rally with an underhand toss to her opponent. Each player gets two touches, ideally a dig and a hit. The player who loses the rally shags the ball and returns to the waiting line. The winner stays and a new player (P) steps on the side where the losing player was, tossing a ball into play to start the next rally. One point is awarded for winning the rally, and an additional point is given if the rally is won using an overhand attack.

Variations: If there are enough players to play on both halves of the court, then the drill becomes a work-up format where, after a certain amount of time, whoever has the lowest amount of points moves down to the other half of the court.

Requirements: Four or more players, a cart of balls and a full court

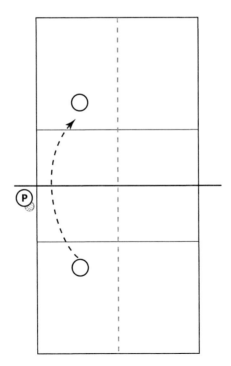

Ball Control
Air Popcorn Machine

Difficulty: ● ○ ○

How it works: Players circle up and start to popcorn (pass to themselves). Once a players ball hits the floor, that ball is out, but the player stays in the drill and wait for another ball from the coach. Coaches can help control the drill by adding volleyballs back into the drill from a toss, so the Air Popcorn Machine is always working! There really is no winning or losing with this drill; the goal is to simply keep the popcorn up and the machine running.

Requirements: Three or more players, a coach, one ball per player and a half court

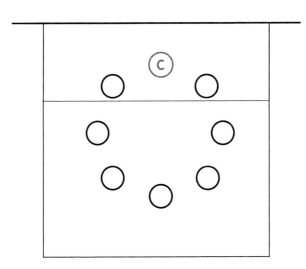

Ball Control
Big Kernel, Little Kernel

Difficulty: ● ● ○

How it works: Each individual starts with a ball. Players bounce the ball back and forth on each arm, starting with a small bounce (little kernel) then a big bounce (big kernel) on one arm before sending the ball over to the other arm. Throughout the drill, players should target their platform sweet spot and continually move their feet to help maintain control of the ball.

Requirements: One or more players, one ball per player and a half court

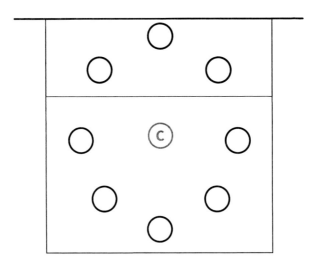

Ball Control
Butterfly

Difficulty: ● ● ●

How it works: This drill has five to seven positions filled on half the floor that create a "modified" butterfly. When done on both halves, it takes the look of butterfly wings. The coach or tosser (T) is positioned 5-15 feet behind the 10-foot line. The tosser tosses to the setter (S). The setter can self-set a couple of times to gain control or a more advanced setter can simply set out to the outside hitter (H). The hitter hits as the blocker (B) goes up to block. The digger (D), who starts deeper in defense, works to dig or get the touch. Hitters are encouraged to hit at the digger. The digger can either turn and shag the ball, or the coach can add a shagger to go get the ball while all other players rotate up a position. Players must learn to follow the pattern of the ball to know where to rotate. With the drill occupying both sides of the floor it does best when it is set up opposite or facing one another again, forming that butterfly appearance.

Requirements: Five or more players, a coach, a cart of balls and a full court

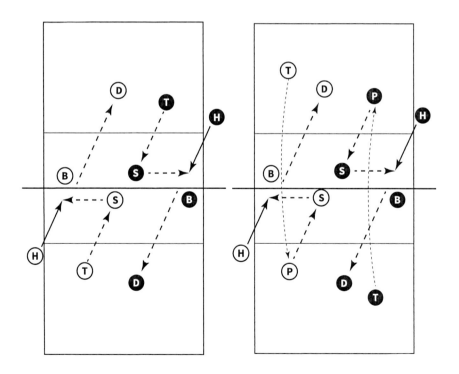

www.theartofcoachingvolleyball.com/youthdb1

Ball Control
Funny Pepper

Difficulty: ● ● ○

How it works: Players pair up and assume a traditional pepper position about 10 feet apart. Player 1 is the attacker (A). Player 2 is the defender (D). Each player starts with a ball in hand. To begin, the defender tosses her ball into the air above her head as the attacker hits a down ball at her. The defender digs her partner's hit, then catches her own ball while the attacker sets to herself and restarts the pattern. Players strive to complete as many patterns as possible without error.

Variations: To speed up play, have the attacker hit the ball every time without a set in between. You can also add a second attacker to the drill to challenge the defender even more.

Requirements: Two players, two balls and 10 feet of court space

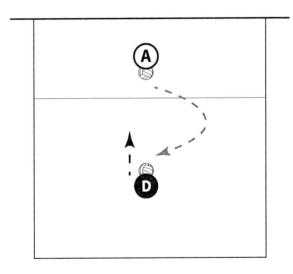

Ball Control
Over-the-Net Pepper

Difficulty: ● ● ●

How it works: Partners are positioned across the net from one another. From a toss over the net, the receiving partner passes, sets, and hits the ball back over to his or her partner. The tosser may catch the ball and start again or can try to also self-pepper. This drill can also be done on one side of the net. Players try to control movements and communicate the skills while keeping the ball going back and forth.

Requirements: Two or more players, one ball per pair and a full court

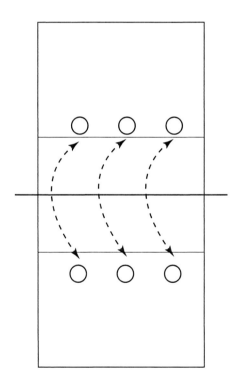

Ball Control
Partner Tennis Ball Tosses

Difficulty: ● ○ ○

How it works:
- **Drill 1:** Grab a partner and line up about five feet apart. Partners toss a tennis ball back and forth using two hands while squatting to toss and receive. The focus is on using the wrist, thumb and hand with arms away from the chest to deliver the toss. This teaches the basics of the pass. Players can add a side step-hop to practice footwork.
- **Drill 2:** Partners toss a tennis ball back and forth, using one hand at a time. Alternate the toss from player 1's right hand to player 2's right hand, then repeat with left hand to left hand.
- **Drill 3:** Partners bounce a tennis ball back and forth, using one hand at a time. Alternate the bounce from right hand to right hand, then left hand to left hand.

Variations: For a greater challenge, give each player a tennis ball and have them one-hand toss or bounce to each other at the same time.

Requirements: Two or more players, one to two tennis balls per pair and a half court

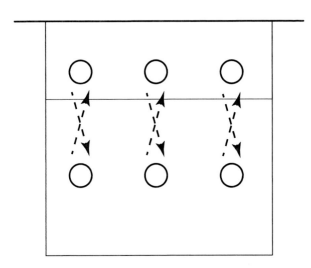

Ball Control
Patterns Drill

Difficulty: ● ● ○

How it works: Coach yells out a series of skills, "Pass to yourself, Pass to your self," "Self-set, self-set," etc., and players all attempt that challenge of patterns. A pattern might be "down ball, pass to yourself, self-set" or perhaps "self-set, pass to yourself."

Variations: Players can partner up and give each other a pattern and the coach has to guess your creative ball handling pattern.

Requirements: One or more players, one ball per player and a half court

www.theartofcoachingvolleyball.com/youthdb1

Ball Control
Popcorn Series

Difficulty: ● ● ○

How it works: Players learn to individually control the ball by "popping," passing to themselves. The quick punch or pop right before contact is the goal. Players have fun alternating their popcorn or by seeing how many consecutive popcorn contacts they can complete.

Variations: Coaches can add to the challenge by adding the one-two-cross move, where players make two contacts on one arm then pop the ball over to make two contacts on the other.

Requirements: One player, one ball and at least 5 feet of court space

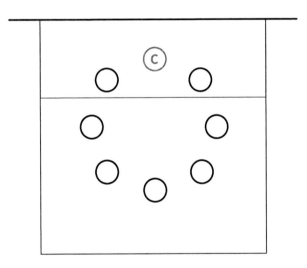

Ball Control
Rotating Group Pepper

Difficulty: ● ● ●

How it works: Divide the court into four quadrants with a right and left quadrant on each side. Assemble three teams of three players, and place each group into a quadrant. The near right quadrant remains empty. To begin, toss a ball to Group 1 in the far right quadrant. That team proceeds to complete three touches with the third one going cross-court to the near left quadrant. Group 1 then rotates clockwise to the open quadrant. At the same time, the group that received the cross-court ball (Group 2) plays its touches, and sends the ball down the line to Group 3 in the far left quadrant. Group 3 executes their touches, sending their third shot cross-court to Group 1. Play continues with each group making three touches on their turn, and sending the ball to the next group in order. Teams should repeat a pattern of cross-court shot and rotate, then line shot and rotate.

Variations: In phase one, each player sets the ball in a set-set-set pattern. In phase two, players advance to a bump-set-spike pattern.

Requirements: Nine players, one ball and a full court

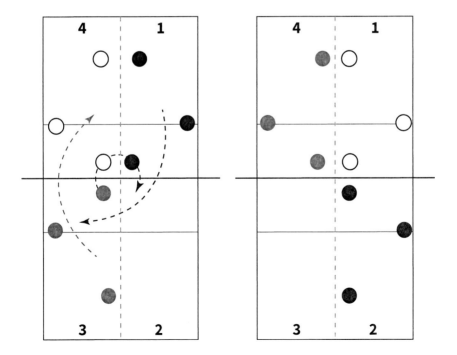

Ball Control
Ten to Kill

Difficulty: ● ● ●

How it works: Players assemble on the court in a 6 vs. 6 formation. To begin, a coach tips the ball to a side and players pass-set-hit the ball to the other team. Since this is a cooperative drill, the intent is not to win the point by going for a kill at this time. Instead, teams must work together to get the ball over the net 10 times. Once that occurs, either team may go for the kill. The team who earns the kill gets a BIG point. Play then resumes with a tip going to the opposing side and both teams once again working together to get the ball over the net 10 times before a kill attempt can be made. The drill continues until one side earns 5 BIG points.

Variations: For younger or less experienced players, reduce the number of times the ball must cross the net before the kill attempt.

Requirements: Twelve players, a coach, a cart of balls and a full court

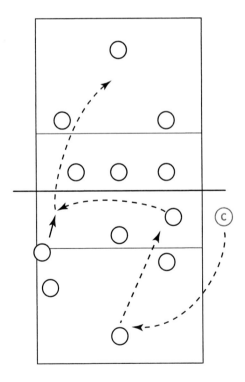

Check out the youth drill videos we have online!

Ball Control
Two Ball Pepper

Difficulty: ● ● ●

How it works: Two players line up facing each other about 10 feet apart. Player 1 is the hitter/catcher/tosser. Player 2 is the digger/setter. Player 1 starts the drill with two balls. Player 1 tosses one ball to player 2 while holding the second one under her arm. Player 2 sets the ball back to player 1. Player 1, still holding the second ball, hits the first ball back to Player 2. Player 2 digs the hit ball. While the ball is in the air, player 1 tosses the second ball to player 2, and the toss-set-hit-dig routine begins again.

Requirements: Two players, two balls and 10 feet of court space

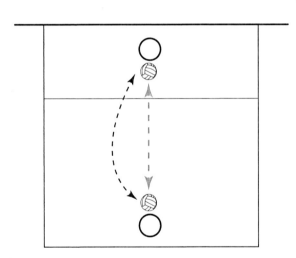

Ball Control
Volleyball Jog

Difficulty: ● ● ○

How it works: The players go for a light and easy jog around the floor - as a team! With a ball under their arm, players stop on a coach's whistle. As they "rest," they perform a series of ball handling challenges such as popcorn, down balls, and self-sets. Once a challenge is over, players go another lap or two, awaiting the whistle for their next task. This is a good ball handling activity.

Requirements: Six or more players, a coach, one ball per player and a full court

Team Drills

Team
7-Up

Difficulty: ● ● ○

How it works: A coach divides the team into groups of three. The three players are: a tosser or setter, a passer and a hitter. The tosser has his or her back on the net, facing the baseline. The passer is in the ready position, waiting to pass. The hitter, depending on whether right- or left-handed, is positioned ready to hit a down ball or hit the ball over the net. The drill begins with a toss, then a pass sends the ball back to the tosser. The tosser sets the ball to the hitter. If the three players successfully accomplish all three skills, players celebrate with a "7-Up!" loud, enthusiastic huddle-out moment. If the three players get the three hits and the ball doesn't go over, the players huddle up for a not-so-enthusiastic "Diet 7-Up" call. The coach can rotate players every 2 to 3 minutes to make sure all players get to play at each position.

Requirements: Six or more players, a coach, one ball per group and a full court

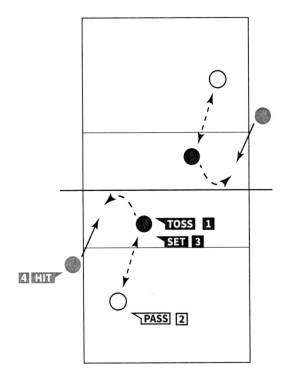

Team
Bad Pass, Good Save

Difficulty: ● ● ○

How it works: Players are positioned in three lines on the baseline. The coach is on the same side of the players with the cart and volleyballs. With six players on the floor, the coach slaps the ball and says, "It's up!" The coach's toss is the first hit, meaning the side of six only has two more contacts to get the ball over the net. The coach's toss is a "bad pass," and the next two hits are the "good saves." This drill is a real game-like drill. It helps prepare the team for a less-than-great first pass. The second hit or first save should be brought back to the middle of the floor, so the team can call out the third hit. The team must survive the bad pass and make something good come out of things. The three diggers on the other side of the net help shag and may play it out, if time permits. Players rotate on the wash call by the coach. Passers move up to the front row, the front row dips under the net and become the new diggers. The old diggers shag any balls that are out, then they hop back in line.

Requirements: Nine or more players, a coach, a cart of balls and a full court

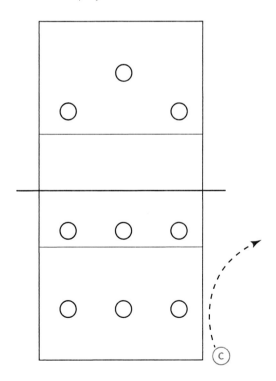

Team
Catch, Toss, Spike Game

Difficulty: ● ● ○

How it works: To warm up for this game, players pair off and toss high balls to each other. The non-tosser runs to get underneath the ball and catch it while positioned in proper hitting alignment.

Next, they play a version of "queen of the court" doubles where they toss the ball to their partner and their partner hits it over the net. The player on the other side who is nearest the ball tries to catch it. If she does, she tosses to her partner, her partner spikes and play continues.

Scoring is up to the coach, but it can look something like this: full point for a spike that goes down, half point for a catch, half point for a ball that's hit over the net but goes out. (It's always better to hit the ball over the net than into the net because there's a chance the other team might play it.)

Requirements: Two or more players, a coach, one ball per group and a full court

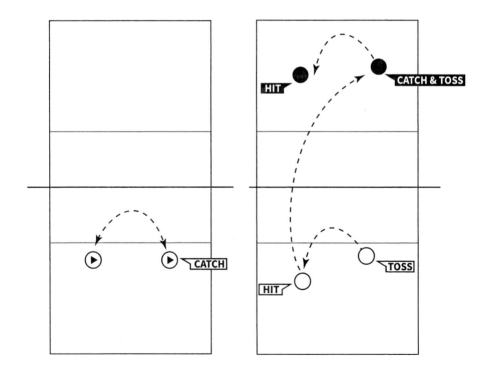

Team
Free Ball, Free Ball, Free Ball, Attack

Difficulty: ● ● ●

How it works: Two coaches are ideal so that there are volleyballs coming from both outside hitting areas. Set up players in a 6 vs. 6 formation to create a scrimmage-like feel. To begin, the first coach tosses a free ball over the net. The defending team transitions from defense to offense as they play out the free ball. Once the ball is dead, play continues as the second coach sends a free ball to the other side. After a third free ball, the final transition is a hard-driven down ball. The team tries to turn this dig into an offense, hitter coverage, then finally back to defense. Players communicate each transition loudly by yelling, "Defense-defense, cover-cover, free-free." The coach can wash the drill or have players rotate a position to ensure all team members are familiar with each position's duties.

Variations: An attack from one coach can be changed into an "adjusted" defense where all balls are played out.

Requirements: Twelve players, two coaches, two carts of balls and a full court

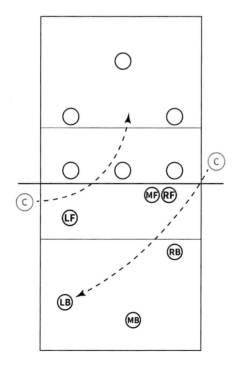

Team
Free Ball, Free Ball, Free Ball, Wash

Difficulty: ● ● ●

How it works: Players line up in three lines on the baseline. Players are sent out to the court in a "wash" drill formation, playing 6 vs. 6, or 3 vs. 3 if there are not enough players. The coach tosses a ball over the net to the side opposite from the three lines (Side A). From the toss, the players play volleyball. After three free ball tosses from the coach, players all yell "Wash!" and rotate up the floor. When players wash off the court, they shag their three volleyballs and return to their lines. An uneven number works fine, the players file in as they come back around the floor to the three lines on the baseline. The team goal and goal for every player should be to be always talking and always moving.

Requirements: Six or more players, a coach, a cart of balls and a full court

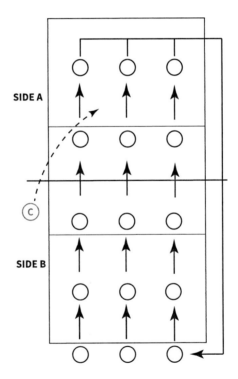

Team
Golden Egg Drill

Difficulty: ● ● ○

How it works: Four players set up for short court with two players on each side of the net. Each pair is given a "golden egg" ball which must not touch the ground. What makes this so hard? The golden eggs aren't the only balls in the drill. The third ball introduced is the ball used for rallying. One team initiates the rally by serving the playing ball over the net. The passer holding their team's golden egg must toss it to their partner before they can pass the playing ball. The rally continues until one team wins the point with the rally volleyball or one team drops their "golden egg." Teams earn one point when they score with the rally volleyball, and two points when the opponent drops their "golden egg" ball.

Requirements: Four players, three balls and a full court

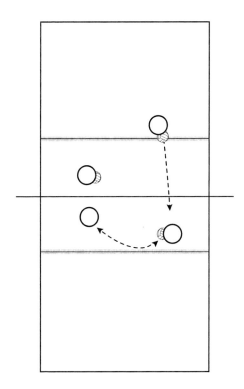

Team
Mini Player Tournament

Difficulty: ● ● ●

How it works: This mini-tournament format pits individual players against each other. Starting with a 1-on-1 round, players battle in 1/3 of skinny court space. Winning players move up while losing players move down. After 10 rounds, points are awarded based on where players finished. For example, a player who finished on the top court earns 10 points while the 2nd place player gets nine points and so on.

In the next round, players draw partner names for 2-on-2 competition, followed by 3-on-3 and on up to 6-on-6. Players continue to earn and track their individual points through each stage of the tournament.

Requirements: Twelve players, six balls and a full court

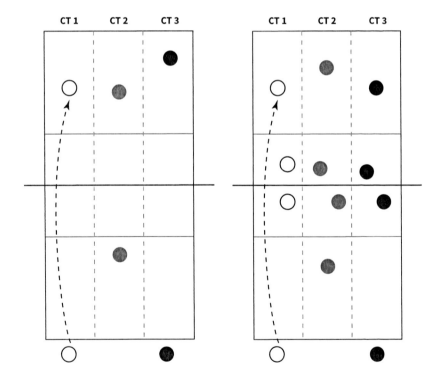

Team
Newcomb Game

Difficulty: ● ● ○

How it works: Players set-up with one player on the winning side and another player on the challenging side with a line of players ready to step onto the court, which is played within the 10-foot (3m) lines. In this "queen of the court" style game, players go head-to-head in three different phases.

- **Phase 1:** Catch and Toss
  To start, two players play short court using only a catch-and-toss technique. Their bodies must face the area they want to hit. The loser goes back in line, and the winner stays to take on the next player.
- **Phase 2:** Catch and Set
  In this phase, players catch the ball, toss it to themselves and set it across the net.
- **Phase 3:** Single Contact
  In the final phase, players are allowed to play just one contact. It can be a pass, set, kick or other type of body contact. No catching is allowed.

Requirements: Two or more players, a coach, a cart of balls and a full court

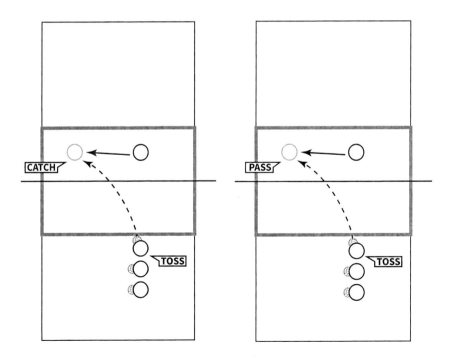

Team
Queens of the Court

Difficulty: ● ● ○

How it works: Players line up in three lines on the baseline while a coach sets up across the net from the Queen side with a cart of volleyballs. The first players in each line are the Queens (Q). As the Queens dip under the net to find the Royal Courtyard, the Princesses (P) step on to challenge them. The coach always tosses across the net to the Queen side. If either side attempts three hits by passing a controlled pass to the setter's zone, the coach grants a life and that team gets a "do over." A life is a way to emphasize three-hit volleyball. When a play ends, new Challengers (CH) come onto the floor and either the Queens remain (if Queens won the point) or new Queens run under the net to take over (if Princesses won the point). Whichever side lost the point always shags the volleyball and returns to their lines. For an uneven number of players encourage new partners.

Requirements: Six or more players, a coach, a cart of balls and a full court

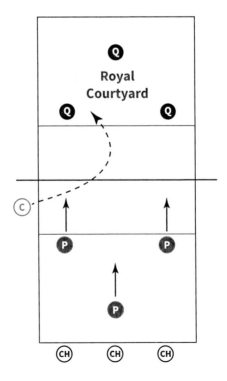

158 Check out the youth drill videos we have online!

Team
Set the Setter

Difficulty: ● ● ○

How it works: In this drill the coach tosses a ball over the net to a passer, the passer uses their hands to over hand pass the ball to the setter who then sets the hitter who swings away. The setter can practice calling his or her sets by saying the name of the hitter being targeted. Players rotate after every touch and the drill repeats.

Variations: Add a second attacker so the setter has two hitters in place: a middle attacker and an outside. Also, if rotating after every touch is too difficult, try rotating after a series of attempts.

Requirements: Six or more players, a coach, a cart of balls and a full court

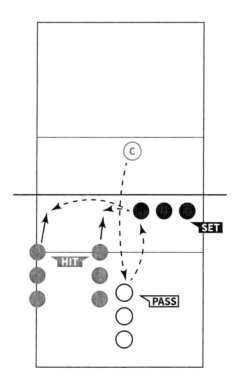

www.theartofcoachingvolleyball.com/youthdb1

Team
Speed Ball

Difficulty: ● ● ○

How it works: Lines on the baseline will organize players for either 3 vs. 3 play or 4 vs. 4 play. Every touch is a point. The coach puts the ball in play with a free ball and players earn up to 3 points on one side, but the ball could be returned for additional points. Players play the free ball toss until it's defined dead and the players wash. The free ball toss always goes to side A. Players keep the same teammates.

Variations: A true three-hits play where the hit goes over the net can result in a bonus 2 points, so the team would get 5 points instead of 3.

Requirements: Six or more players, a coach, a cart of balls and a full court

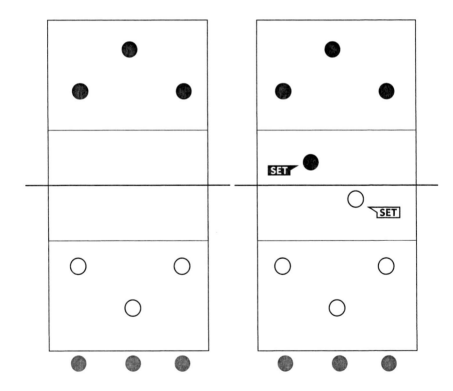